MW00561449

Entering the
OLD TESTAMENT

MEETING
[GOD]
in
Scripture

Entering the

OLD TESTAMENT

LEADER'S
GUIDE

MARY LOU REDDING

UPPER
ROOM BOOKS®
NASHVILLE

Cover design: Jade Novak, Anderson Design Group
Cover photo: Shutterstock, iStockPhoto, Photos.com
First printing: 2007

LIBRARY OF CONGRESS CATALOGING-IN-PUBLICATION DATA

Meeting God in Scripture: entering the Old Testament leader's guide / Mary Lou Redding.
p. cm.
ISBN 978-0-8358-9946-8
1. Bible. O.T.—Devotional use. 2. Bible. O.T.—Study and teaching. 3. Spiritual life—Biblical teaching. I. Meeting God in Scripture. II. Title.
BS1151.55.R43   2007b
221.071—dc22   2007030099

Printed in the United States of America

Contents

Introduction

*W*elcome to *Meeting God in Scripture: Entering the Old Testament.* For the next eight weeks, you will be leading an exploration of Hebrew scripture. What we often refer to as the "Old Testament," scholars and teachers now commonly call "Hebrew scripture" (and sometimes the "First Testament"). This designation is meant to honor these foundational books. It places them not in contrast to or inferior to the New Testament but as valuable in themselves.

This study of Hebrew scripture builds on daily Bible readings (five per week) and personal exploration exercises (entry points) tied to the daily readings. The theme of the study emphasizes humanity's creation for relationship with God. Nothing else can satisfy us. All of scripture records God's commitment to this relationship in spite of our sin, resistance, and even running from God who loves us and who continually reaches out to us.

The daily Bible readings and responses require ten to fifteen minutes a day, and they lead up to and become the starting point for a weekly small-group meeting. This leader's guide includes a process and resources for an introductory meeting and eight weekly meetings of either 45 or 90 minutes. The time for the introductory meeting may vary, depending on how many persons attend and how many community-building activities you include.

Each element of the session has a suggested time frame for a group size of nine. A larger group will be unable to complete the activities in the suggested time. If you attempt to discuss in the whole group rather than in smaller groups of three, time will not allow completion of the activities. Therefore, we strongly encourage you to limit each group to no more than nine persons and to discuss in groups of three. For a larger group, you will need to reduce the time spent on each element or omit a portion from the session plan.

In the introductory meeting, you will present the approach, process, and content of the remaining sessions. The primary difference between this resource and traditional Bible studies is its spiritual-formation approach. To many participants, this approach may seem a dramatic departure from the analytical, left-brain methods that often characterize Bible study. Therefore, the introductory meeting will acquaint participants with the difference between formational and informational reading of the Bible. Meetings in the 90-minute format will include group *lectio divina* (contemplation of and individual response to scripture) in each session; the 45-minute format does *not* include group *lectio* each week. This accounts for the time difference between the two formats. Detailed directions for leading *lectio divina* follow this introduction. They will help you guide the group, and you may also use this information to create a computer presentation to aid your teaching.

Customizing the 90-minute Format for Your Group

The first 90-minute session includes get-acquainted activities, an introduction to lectio divina, and a group exploration of a scripture passage (EXPLORING THE WORD). Each session (after the introductory session) includes these components:

- Opening
- Interacting with the Word (in triads)
- Exploring the Word (group activity)
- Engaging the Word (*lectio divina*, 90-minute format only)
- Closing

At the end of this guide you will find short introductions to the books of Hebrew scripture that are used in this resource, written from a spiritual-formation perspective. To prepare to lead each week, read the introductions to the books of the Bible you and participants will study that week. Reading the article "What Is Spiritual Formation?" (page 97) will ready you for the introductory session's exploration activity.

Preparing the Meeting Space

The activities in this study aim to involve participants on sensory and affective levels. A welcoming and worshipful atmosphere serves to reinforce those experiences. You may set up a worship center on a small table, using seasonal decorations that change weekly. Or you may develop a worship center with a Christ candle, a cross, and other symbols. A group member may have special gifts for creating such worship arrangements. During the introductory session, ask for volunteers who would prepare the worship center weekly.

Music adds greatly to the sessions. If you cannot lead singing, ask for a volunteer from the group to help with music/singing during opening and closing worship and prayer times. Compile a list of appropriate songs from the songbooks and hymnals available in your meeting place, and give these to the music leader before the first session. You may want to use the same hymn, chorus, or song to begin and end a session, so that you need to choose only eight.

Each session will include conversation in groups of three about the week's readings and entry-point responses, so a setting in which chairs move easily from a circle arrangement (for OPENING and the large-group discussion of INTERACTING WITH THE WORD) into triads (for small-group discussion) would be advantageous.

When sessions include handouts, placing these on chairs or tables before participants arrive reduces confusion and creates a more peaceful atmosphere. If you plan to use a computer presentation, check it out before each session to reduce technological problems, confusion, and wasted time.

Looking Ahead: Supplies/Special Arrangements

All sessions:	Always have on hand, newsprint or whiteboard and markers, extra Bibles, paper and writing utensils, name tags.
Intro session:	The introductory session calls for modeling clay or play dough for each participant.
Session 4:	The experiential activity calls for small globes or balls or color pictures of the world—perhaps a photo of Earth taken from space—for each participant.
Session 7:	This session invites you to use your church sanctuary for the experiential activity, so you will need to arrange accordingly.
Session 8:	You will need multiple copies of the local-news and international-news sections from the newspaper.

Leading Lectio Divina in Groups (for 90-minute sessions)

Lectio divina is a Latin phrase often translated as "spiritual reading" or "holy reading." But for the first fifteen hundred years of the Christian church, people learned and absorbed the words and stories of scripture by *hearing* them read. Scrolls and books were rare, and most people could not read. Personal copies of the Bible in the language of ordinary life were not available until long after the invention of the printing press in the late 1400s, and even then only to the wealthy. So when we hear scripture being read, we sit in company with the first saints who listened to hear God's personal word to them through the words of the Bible.

If you have never led *lectio divina* in a small group, the process outlined here may seem too simple to be effective. Please trust the approach. In just a few sessions you will see God at work as participants grow in their eagerness and ability to hear God speak to them through the words of scripture. Those who tested this resource emphasized that the group reflection on scripture was an invaluable part of the design. The time investment is worth the return for the participants. For more background on *lectio divina*, read "Meeting God in Scripture" (page 103).

Lectio divina is based on hearing a passage of scripture read several times. Using the directions below, you will guide group members in listening, reflecting in silence, talking with others, and praying in response to what they have heard. Allowing silence may be the most difficult part of the process for both leader and participants. Don't rush the silence; use a watch with a second hand to be sure you allow ample time for each step.

Preparing the Group to Listen

Before the first session of *lectio divina*, you may want to reflect together on "Obstacles to Hearing God in Scripture" (page 14) as group members think about all the things we do instead of listening—analyzing, classifying, and so on. The first two steps in the *lectio* process may be the most demanding because they require listening and silence. In the first step, you will invite group members to listen for a word or phrase from the Bible passage you read and to consider it in silence. The second tough step comes when you direct them to repeat *only* that word or phrase within their small group. They speak it aloud without comment or elaboration.

We are so accustomed to analyzing, to stepping back from scripture to *think about* what it means, that we often do not listen to the words themselves. For instance, if we read aloud the story of the persistent widow from Luke 18:1-8, some people will think and say within their group the word *perseverance*. But that word does not appear in the passage. That word and others like it (*compassion, mercy, faith*) are thoughts about the passage, and they reflect our analysis rather than the words we actually heard. Try to help group members realize that they are to listen for a word or phrase that occurs in the passage, not come up with a word to *describe* the passage. They are not to step back to analyze or categorize the reading.

Before you begin, invite group members to sit in groups of three, to become comfortable, and to prepare for a time of listening to scripture. Tell them that they will be hearing a passage of scripture—the same passage—read several times and that each reading will be followed by silence for reflection. Ask them to trust you to guide them through the process. Suggest that they give themselves fully to hearing the scripture—not reading along in their own Bibles but listening.

On the third reading, a group member will read the passage aloud so participants will hear it at least once in a voice other than yours. Ask for a volunteer to do this before beginning. Read the passage from the same translation each time to avoid distracting people by differences between the translations. You may want to photocopy from your Bible the page containing each session's *lectio divina* passage and mark the reading to make the change of readers less intrusive and to be sure the same translation is used. Tell the participants that the small groups will not be "reporting" to the entire body in any way and that what they say within their smaller groups will remain private.

The Process for Group *Lectio Divina*

STEP ONE: (first-stage reading) Tell the group that you will read the passage twice, once to orient them to its overall content and then again, more slowly, so that they can listen for a word or phrase that stops them or gets their attention. Read the passage aloud, twice.

In the silence, repeat your word or phrase to yourself and reflect on it.

Allow one to two minutes of silence. (*Time this step so you do not rush.*)

STEP TWO: **Within your group, repeat the word or phrase that attracted you—without comment, summary, or analysis. (Or you may pass.)**

STEP THREE: (second-stage reading) Ask group members to listen as you read the passage again, slowly, being open to how it connects to them. (Tell them that their word or phrase may or may not be the same one on this reading as during the first reading.)

In silence, consider how your word or phrase connects to your life right now—a situation, a feeling, a possibility.

Allow three minutes of silence for reflection.

STEP FOUR: (At this point, tell the group that at any time participants may always choose not to speak by saying "pass" when their turn comes.)

In your groups, take a few minutes each to tell about the connection you sense between your life and your word or phrase. (Or you may pass.)

Ask the person closest to you in each group to be the first speaker.

STEP FIVE: (third-stage reading) Ask the alternate reader to read the passage again, slowly. Invite group members to listen during this reading for an invitation from God for the next few days:

In the silence, consider what invitation you hear from God. Be open to a sensory impression, an image, a song, a fragrance.

Allow three minutes of silence for reflection.

STEP SIX: Ask group members to ponder in silence the invitation they heard. Allow several minutes of silence.

STEP SEVEN: Invite each person to speak about the invitation he or she senses from God for his or her life in the next few days:

In your groups, allow each person to tell about the invitation he or she heard. (Or you may pass.)

This time, have the person farthest from you to begin. This is an important step in the process, so allow ample time for each person to speak. Watch the groups; check to see which are finishing up, which need more time. Do not rush the process.

STEP EIGHT: Invite persons to pray for each other, one by one in turn, within their smaller groups. Ask each one to pray for the person to his or her right. The group members can decide whether they will pray aloud or silently.

Pray for each other to be empowered to respond to the invitations you heard. (You may pray silently or aloud.)

Remind participants to remain silent when their group finishes praying, since other groups may still be in prayer. When all have finished praying, say "amen" to end the process.[1]

You may want to debrief this experience of *lectio divina* by asking the group as a whole to comment on it: What worked for them? What was difficult about this way of responding to scripture? Have they been led through this process before, and, if so, what was different, better, or worse about it this time? This would be a good time to mention that everyone responds differently to the various ways of exploring scripture and that there is no expected outcome.

Obstacles to Hearing God in Scripture

Common obstacles:

- thinking/talking about scripture

- classifying

- comparing

- describing

- explaining

- looking for "the lesson" rather than listening to scripture:

  the actual words that are there

  the emotions we feel

  the connections we make

  the memories that arise

Informational and Formational Reading

Reading for information is an integral part of teaching and learning. But reading is also concerned with listening for the special guidance, for the particular insight, for your relationship with God. What matters is the attitude of mind and heart.

Informational Reading

1. Informational reading is concerned with covering as much material as possible and as quickly as possible.

2. Informational reading is linear—seeking an objective meaning, truth, or principle to apply.

3. Informational reading seeks to master the text.

4. In informational reading, the text is an object out there for us to control.

5. Informational reading is analytical, critical, and judgmental.

6. Informational reading is concerned with problem solving.

Formational Reading

1. Formational reading is concerned with small portions of content rather than quantity.

2. Formational reading focuses on depth and seeks multiple layers of meaning in a single passage.

3. Formational reading allows the text to master the student.

4. Formational reading sees the student as the object to be shaped by the text.

5. Formational reading requires a humble, detached, willing, loving approach.

6. Formational reading is open to mystery. Students come to the scripture to stand before the Mystery called God and to let the Mystery address them.

Adapted from information in *Shaped by the Word: The Power of Scripture in Spiritual Formation*, rev. ed., by M. Robert Mulholland Jr. (Nashville, TN.: Upper Room Books, 2000), 49–63. Used by permission of Upper Room Books.

Permission is granted to make one copy for each participant.

Being Shaped by God

Preparing for the introductory session: Read the article "What Is Spiritual Formation?" (leader's guide, page 97) and the article "Reading Scripture Devotionally" in the participant's workbook (page 11). Reading the article "Meeting God in Community" (page 107) will also help you set the stage for a meaningful small-group experience. Look over the chart that compares informational and formational approaches to reading scripture (page 15).

Note important ideas from the articles. Read through the introductory session plan until you feel comfortable leading it, especially the reading from Genesis and the reflection on it. You will need to tailor this session to fit your time frame. An alternate approach to the introductions is provided. Other places to save time might include passing out materials without a great deal of discussion.

Materials Needed

- Worship center (Christ candle, means to light it)
- Participant's workbooks. Since group members will be writing or drawing in the books as part of the daily reflection, each person will need her or his own copy.
- Name tags and markers

- Newsprint or whiteboard and markers
- Modeling clay or play dough for each participant
- Extra Bibles for those who may not have brought theirs
- Copies (one for each participant) of "Informational and Formational Reading" (page 15) and "Obstacles to Hearing God in Scripture" (page 14)

Opening (5 minutes)

Welcome persons as they arrive. Distribute the participant's workbooks as part of your greeting, and invite folks to browse through them until the session begins.

Light the candle and tell the group you light it as a reminder that the One who created light—and us—is present with us in this study to shed light on all we will do.

Read Genesis 1:1-3a. Invite the group members to mention aloud other good things that they have experienced this week. Offer a prayer of gratitude for all God's good gifts to us, especially the gift of being able to study scripture together.

Sing a hymn or chorus.

Building Community (20 minutes)

Welcome participants to the study. Explain that they'll receive more information about what to expect during the coming weeks, later in the session, after they get to know one another better.

Introductions: Invite group members to pair off by finding a person they do not know or the person they know least well in the group. Tell them that, after conversation, they will introduce each other to the group. Give the pairs six minutes to get to know each other (signal when three minutes has passed). Suggest nonthreatening questions to ask, such as how they came to attend this church, where they live, where they went to school, what denomination they grew up in. *Add one specific question*: What is one fact about you that probably no one else in the room knows? After six minutes, invite the pairs to introduce each other to the rest of the group based on their conversation. Give the speakers one or two minutes each for the introductions, depending on the size of the group.

Alternate introductions for 45-minute session (10 minutes): Have persons introduce themselves. Give people one minute to say whatever they want about themselves, including one fact about them that no one in the room knows.

Establishing a Group Agreement (10 minutes)

Most small groups operate with an agreement that includes points such as these:

Presence: Attend each meeting unless serious reasons keep you away.

Prayer: Between meeting times, group members pray for one another and for the group's endeavors together.

Preparation: Group members make the daily readings and exercises a priority, doing them as diligently as life allows.

Participation: Group members will participate honestly and openly in the activities of the sessions.

Confidentiality: What is said within the group remains in the group. Members will not discuss outside the group anything others say within this setting.

Courtesy: Group members will listen to one another with respect and without interrupting or engaging in side conversations. When opinions differ, group members will not attempt to persuade anyone to any point of view but will listen for what God may be saying in the differences.

Post the words *presence, prayer, preparation, participation, confidentiality,* and *courtesy* on newsprint or a board. Mention what each means for this group and ask if folks want to accept these definitions or add to or modify them. You may want to display reminders of your group's agreement in the meeting room each time you gather.

Introducing the Study (20 minutes)

Be sure all participants have a copy of the workbook.

Explain that this study of the Bible will probably differ from other studies folks may have participated in. There will be no memorizing or outlining. Have participants open their workbooks to page 26, to the entry point related to session 2, day 2. Give them time to read the suggested guided response to Leviticus 13:45-46. Ask, "Based on looking at this process, how does this way of studying the Bible compare to other studies you have participated in?" List the responses on newsprint.

Next, direct the attention of the group to the article "Reading Scripture Devotionally" (page 11, participant's workbook). Give the members time to read the article. After five minutes, check to see if everyone is finished and allow more time as necessary. When they have completed the reading, ask them to compare the article's ideas to their responses listed on the newsprint. Where do their ideas echo the article? Where do their ideas differ from those in the article? What questions or concerns did the article raise for them? Respond to questions. If you don't have an answer to someone's concern, invite group members to respond.

Explain that the ideas in the article shape this study. This study will not attempt to survey the entire Old Testament. Each day participants will read a portion of scripture. Then they will read again, looking closely at one verse or a few verses from the passage. They will respond to the verse or verses by following the process suggested in each "entry point." Each day's reading and activity will take only ten to fifteen minutes to complete.

The "starred" entry point: One of each week's five entry points has two stars alongside the title. (Direct them to page 22—session 1, day 4) to show them a starred article. Ask group members to make time to do the starred activity each week even if they are too crunched for time to do them all, because this activity will be part of the weekly group meeting.

Direct their attention to the section of the introduction titled "If You Want to Do More: Keeping a Spiritual Journal" (page 9), and talk about keeping a journal. Ask if any in the group have kept a journal. If so, invite these persons to tell the group the benefits they received from the practice. Emphasize that journals are private and no one will be asked to reveal anything he or she has written.

Exploring the Word (15 minutes)

Distribute the modeling clay or play dough. Encourage group members to begin manipulating the clay, shaping and reshaping it.

Explain that you will read some passages from Genesis to the group and you want them to work the clay as they listen. Ask them to notice the temperature of the clay, its pliability, its weight, and then to begin to knead it, gently and firmly. Then ask them to think of a shape and to begin to form the clay into that shape while you read.

Read aloud Genesis 1:1-31 and 2:1-8. Read Genesis 2:1-8 a second time, more slowly. When you finish reading, allow folks several minutes to finish their clay creations. Then direct them to the entry point for Genesis 2:7 (page 15, participant's workbook). Ask them to take two minutes to write responses as suggested in the entry point.

Invite group members to talk about what they think the term *spiritual formation* means in light of working with the clay. Remind them that the Bible readings and entry-point responses in this study provide spiritual-formation opportunities by helping us attend to God's work in our lives as we become conformed to the image of Christ.

Discussion: Formational Versus Informational Reading (15 minutes)

Distribute copies of the chart comparing the two ways of reading the Bible and other Christian resources. Talk about the entries on the chart and help group members compare the two approaches. Point out that our educational system concentrates on helping students develop left-brain, analytical skills and often presents education as a linear process focusing on cognitive abilities. For example, ask participants to think about the difference between attitudes about art classes and math classes in an average school or about our constant quantifying (grades, reports, assessments) rather than relational focus in educating. We will be approaching scripture as an opportunity to encounter God and learn about ourselves and one another.

Closing (5 minutes)

Invite group members to voice their wishes and hopes about this course and the group's time together.

Pray, offering to God all the hopes and wishes expressed and asking for God's help in listening and responding with heart, soul, mind, and strength.

Ask for volunteers who might be willing to assist in music selection and singing or those who might enjoy helping set up the worship center each week.

Preparing for Session 1

- Complete the daily readings and entry-point responses in the participant's workbook.
- Read the introductions to the books of Genesis and Exodus.
- Review the process for leading *lectio divina* until you feel comfortable using it, and photocopy and mark the passage for the alternate reader.
- Provide name tags and markers.
- Prepare materials for the worship center.

Created for

Relationship

NOTE: All meeting outlines are for 90-minute sessions; if you are using this study in a 45-minute session, you will need to abbreviate or adapt the opening and closing portions and omit the *lectio divina* experience.

Have name tags and markers available every week.

Opening (8 minutes)

Light the candle and tell the group you do so as a reminder that the God whose word in scripture lights our path is with us now as we study.

As a part of worship and to continue getting to know one another, invite the group members to share their earliest memory of reading or studying the Bible.

Sing a hymn, song, or chorus about the Bible.

Close this time by praying a prayer of thanks for all those who have brought us to this study, in whatever ways they had a part.

Interacting with the Word (17 minutes)

Below are several questions the smaller groups (triads) might use when discussing each week's Bible reading and responses. Choose two of the questions for discussion this week and gauge the group's response to them. You may use the same questions each week or vary them.

Before the discussion begins in the smaller groups, allow people a couple of minutes to review their comments and daily responses to the Bible readings in their participant's workbook. Encourage group members to listen for God in each person's words. Remind everyone to allow each group member time to respond to a question before the group moves on to the next.

Some possible questions:

- What scripture reading and accompanying entry point drew the most response?
- What scripture reading and entry-point activity most surprised you?
- What did you learn through the week's readings?
- What insight did you connect with your life?
- What persons or ideas touched on this week would you like to know more about?
- What reading most challenged you?
- What questions do you have about the week's readings?
- What relationships do you see differently because of the week's readings and responses?
- How did your actions or attitudes change in response to the daily Bible readings?

    If you prefer, use your own questions.

Group Discussion (5 minutes)

Ask the group as a whole to respond:

- How did the process go for you this week with the Bible reading and entry-point responses?
- How many people in your small group had similar responses? Which ones?
- What questions or concerns do you want to bring to the group?

Deal with process questions by answering or clarifying as you can.

Exploring the Word (15 minutes)

This activity builds on the entry point for Exodus 3:1-12. Invite the group to retell the Bible story of Moses' encounter with the burning bush by having each person say one sentence about it.

Compare the callings of Moses and Samuel. Ask participants to open their Bibles and read 1 Samuel 3:1-10. In groups of three, have them compare and contrast God's encounter with Moses and with Samuel. On newsprint or a board, list differences between the two calls in one column and likenesses between them in another. (You may want to point out that often in the Bible, as with Moses, fire or light are part of encounter with God: Isaiah and the burning coals that touched his lips, Paul and the blinding light, Samuel and the lamp in the Temple, the Hebrew boys in the fiery furnace. Even after the "quiet" encounter with Christ on the road to Emmaus, the travelers say, looking back, "Didn't our hearts burn within us as he spoke to us on the way?"

Ask group members to reflect on whether they are more like Moses (naturally aware of God directly and clearly) or more like Samuel (need a mentor like Eli to help them understand their experience of God's call)? Allow silence for them to consider this. Ask which way of encountering God they think is more common, and why. If you have more time, ask group members to explore the positives of the way that is not theirs and to state why they see them as positives.

Start a new list and ask group members to mention some unspectacular ways God reaches into our lives.

Finally, invite participants silently to identify ways they have experienced God coming into their lives in the past week. Give them time to record these in their workbook.

Engaging the Word (lectio divina, 45 minutes)

Use the steps outlined for leading group *lectio* to guide the group through contemplation of **Genesis 28:10-17**.

Closing (5 minutes)

Close your time together by asking participants to voice any insights they had during the session about experiencing God's presence. Model this by mentioning an insight you had either while preparing or during the session.

Invite participants to reflect in silence on this: **What "word from the LORD" do you take from this session into the coming week?**

Sing a song, hymn, or chorus that affirms God's constant presence with us. Send the group forth with this benediction: **Go in peace, with the assurance that God goes with you. Amen.**

Preparing for Session 2

- Complete the daily readings and entry-point responses in the participant's workbook.

- Read the introductions to the books of Exodus, Leviticus, Numbers, and Deuteronomy.

- Review the process for leading *lectio divina* until you feel comfortable using it; photocopy and mark the passage for the alternate reader.

- Prepare a poster, list on newsprint, or make handouts of the Ten Commandments as they appear in Deuteronomy 5, using the verses indicated in the fifth reading in the participant's workbook. (See page 29 for a reproducible sheet.)

- Prepare sheets with selected commandments for each small group to work on in the EXPLORING THE WORD activity.

- Prepare materials for the worship center.

Holy Ground

NOTE: All meeting outlines are for 90-minute sessions; if you are using this study in a 45-minute session, you will need to abbreviate or adapt the opening and closing portions and omit the *lectio divina* experience.

Opening (5 minutes)

Light the candle and tell the group you do so as a reminder that God is present, and therefore they are on holy ground. Read aloud Joshua 5:13-15 and ask participants to reflect in silence on times when they have experienced a sense of standing on "holy ground" or whether a place can be made to seem holy and what makes it so. Ask them to name places where they have felt God's presence. Close by giving thanks for these times and places in their lives.

Sing a hymn or chorus such as "I Want to Walk as a Child of the Light," "Sweet, Sweet Spirit," or another appropriate song to set the tone of the session.

Interacting with the Word (15 minutes)

Form groups of three. Use the same questions as last week or choose new ones from the list. Give time for review of responses in the participant's workbook before discussion begins. Write the questions you'll be using on a board or flip chart. Once again, encourage group members to listen for God in the responses of others in their small group.

Exploring the Word (20 minutes)

This activity builds on the entry point for Deuteronomy 5:1-21 (day 5). See listing of commandments on page 29 of this leader's guide.

The group will cooperatively write questions based on each of the Ten Commandments to create a process for self-evaluation, according to the pattern suggested in the entry point. Form smaller groups and choose commandments from parts of the list for each group (since the first commandments are longer and more involved than the later ones). For example, with three groups, assign group one to work with commandments number 1, 4, and 7. Assign group two to work with commandments 2, 5, and 8. Assign group three to work with commandments 3, 6, 9, and 10.

Give each group time to write its questions and then use them as a litany of self-evaluation. Have the questions read aloud in the order of the commandments, pausing for about 30 seconds of silent reflection after each one.

Engaging the Word (lectio divina, 45 minutes)

Use the steps outlined in the section on leading group *lectio* to guide the group through contemplation of **Psalm 103:8-14**.

Closing (5 minutes)

Invite each person to name the gift and the challenge of this session.

Sing a hymn, song, or chorus that affirms God's goodness and unfailing mercy.

Invite a volunteer to pray a closing prayer, or offer one yourself.

The Ten Commandments

(Deuteronomy 5:6-8, 11-12, 16-21)

(1) I am the Lord your God, who brought you out of the land of Egypt, out of the house of slavery; you shall have no other gods before me.

(2) You shall not make for yourself an idol, whether in the form of anything that is in heaven above, or that is on the earth beneath, or that is in the water under the earth.

(3) You shall not make wrongful use of the name of the Lord your God, for the Lord will not acquit anyone who misuses his name.

(4) Observe the sabbath day and keep it holy, as the Lord your God commanded you.

(5) Honor your father and your mother, as the Lord your God commanded you, so that your days may be long and that it may go well with you in the land that the Lord your God is giving you.

(6) You shall not murder.

(7) Neither shall you commit adultery.

(8) Neither shall you steal.

(9) Neither shall you bear false witness against your neighbor.

(10) Neither shall you covet your neighbor's wife.

　　Neither shall you desire your neighbor's house, or field, or male or female slave, or ox, or donkey, or anything that belongs to your neighbor.

Permission is granted to make one copy for each participant.

Preparing for Session 3

- Complete the daily readings and entry-point responses in the participant's workbook.

- Read the introductions to the books of Joshua, Judges, Ruth, and First and Second Samuel.

- Review the process for leading *lectio divina* until you feel comfortable using it; photocopy and mark the passage for the alternate reader.

- Prepare materials for the worship center.

For All

the Saints

NOTE: All meeting outlines are for 90-minute sessions; if you are using this study in a 45-minute session, you will need to abbreviate or adapt the opening and closing portions and omit the *lectio divina* experience.

Opening (5 minutes)

Light the candle and remind the group as you do so that its light signifies Christ's presence with us.

Invite group members to name their favorite Bible character and say why this person is special to them.

Sing a song, hymn, or chorus about the company of God's people, such as "I Sing a Song of the Saints of God" or another of your choosing.

Close with a prayer of thanks for those who teach us about being God's people.

Interacting with the Word (15 minutes)

Form groups of three. Post your selected questions from the list provided on page 24 of this leader's guide. Give time for review of responses in participant's workbook before discussion begins. Once again, encourage group members to listen for God in the responses of others in their small group.

Exploring the Word (20 minutes)

This activity builds on the entry point for 2 Samuel 23:8-39 (day 5), using the participants' "halls of fame" on day 5. Give them a moment to review their lists.

Invite group members to tell about one person they have known who is on their list and one Bible character who is on their list and why each is there. If you have time, allow each person in the group to do this.

After all have spoken or time is nearly up, ask group members to think about what characteristics or actions they heard mentioned more than once. Invite them to name these and begin a list on the board or on newsprint of what makes people heroes to one another or of how we influence others.

As the final step in the activity, ask group members to think about the people they see every day or often. Ask them to reflect in silence on their last meeting with two or three of these persons and to consider how they influence these persons' lives.

End the silence by praying a prayer of thanks for those who have formed us and for our heightened awareness of our influence on others.

Engaging the Word (lectio divina, 45 minutes)

Use the steps outlined in the section on leading group *lectio* to guide the group through contemplation of **1 Samuel 1:4-11** or **1 Samuel 2:1-4**.

Closing (5 minutes)

Read aloud Hebrews 11:23-34 and invite group members to name "saints" they have known who are not famous but are important to them. Close this time by asking participants to name characteristics of godly leaders that they want to exhibit in their interactions with others in the coming week.

Sing a hymn or chorus such as "Sanctuary" or another song about being God's presence in the world.

Pray a prayer asking God to help participants to influence others in ways that will draw them and those around them closer to God.

Preparing for Session 4

- Complete the daily readings and entry-point responses in the participant's workbook.

- Read the introductions to the books of First and Second Kings, First and Second Chronicles, Ezra, and Nehemiah.

- Review the process for leading *lectio divina* until you feel comfortable using it; photocopy and mark the passage for the alternate reader.

- Gather balls, world globes, or pictures of Earth from space, one per participant. (Look in school supply stores or on the internet.)

- Read through the group activity (prayer meditation) several times, until you feel comfortable about leading the group in the process.

- Prepare materials for the worship center.

Loving and *Healing*

NOTE: All meeting outlines are for 90-minute sessions; if you are using this study in a 45-minute session, you will need to abbreviate or adapt the opening and closing portions and omit the *lectio divina* experience.

Opening (5 minutes)

Light the Christ candle and say, **We light this candle to remind us that Christ calls us to be the light of the world.**

Read aloud Micah 4:1-3, and invite group members to reflect in silence for a few moments. Then invite sentence prayers growing out of that reflection. Close with a prayer of your own.

Sing a hymn or chorus such as "Here I Am, Lord" or another song appropriate to the tone of the session.

Interacting with the Word (15 minutes)

Form small groups of three. Select questions from the list provided on page 24, and post them on the board or newsprint. Give time for review of responses in the participant's workbook before discussion begins. Once again, encourage group members to listen for God in the responses of others in their small group.

Exploring the Word (20 minutes)

This activity builds on the entry point for 2 Kings 17:5-8 (day 2).

Begin by asking participants to review the entry point for day 2 of the week. Invite them to name the countries and conflicts that came to mind; list these where everyone can see them. Then ask them to name other problems caused by the wars going on in the world. List these as well.

You will be leading the group in a guided prayer meditation, a time of praying for our war-torn world.[2] As you read the meditation, pause at each ellipsis (. . .) to allow time for images to form in hearers' minds and hearts. Read through the meditation several times and do the steps yourself as a way to gauge how long the pauses should be.

Introduce the experience by saying something like this: **We are going to enter into a guided prayer experience. I will lead you through this time of prayer by suggesting images to you. There is no right or wrong way to do this, so don't worry about what you do or do not experience. Some people have trouble creating images in their minds; if that is the case with you, just use your mind to think about the places and ideas mentioned.**

Distribute the small globes, balls, or photos and ask group members to quiet themselves and become comfortable as you begin.

The Meditation

While holding the globe (or photo) in their hands, invite the group members to listen to these words from the prophet Isaiah's vision of God's desire for our world:

> **They will not hurt or destroy**
> **on all my holy mountain;**
> **for the earth will be full of the knowledge of the LORD**
> **as the waters cover the sea (11:4).**

Now, relax and let your body become quiet. Breathe deeply, taking in God's own breath of life. . . . Close your eyes and picture or sense the warm light of God's love flowing toward you. . . . Allow this light to fill you, beginning at your head and slowly penetrating every cell of your body. . . . Remember that God created this world and you and said that it is all good, . . . you are good, "fearfully and wonderfully made." . . . Picture this wonderful world with its continents . . . its seas, rivers, brooks . . . its forests . . . deserts . . . plains . . . mountains. . . . See the clouds. . . . See the Earth, this fragile globe suspended in the darkness of space. . . . Sense God's gracious goodness present with us. . . . Now become aware of your concern for the world flowing from your heart . . . feel your love for the Earth, its creatures, its peoples. . . . Sense its needs, hurts, griefs, and hopes . . . hold the world in your hands. . . . See Christ's hands covering your own, cradling the world . . . . see the world lifted into God's mercy. . . . Envision the radiant light of God's healing love surrounding the world. . . . And now, let your mind like a zoom lens go to a part of the world that you know has a special need for prayer. . . . See the place, the people. . . . Feel your concern and God's concern radiating toward that place. . . . See God's Spirit hovering there. . . . See hope and healing growing stronger. . . . See light dawning for that place, and feel God's healing power moving through every part of it. . . . Once you see hope filling that place, let your mind go to another part of the world that you know has a special need for prayer. . . . See the place, the people. . . . Feel your concern and God's concern radiating toward that place. . . . See hope and healing growing stronger. . . . See light dawning for that place, and feel God's healing power moving through every part of it. . . . Once you see hope filling that place, move to another part of the world that you know has a special need for prayer. . . . See the place, the people. . . . Feel your concern and God's concern radiating toward that place. . . . See hope and healing growing stronger. . . . See light dawning for that place, and feel God's healing power moving through every part of it. . . . Moving back out to the wider view, see again the entire planet. . . . Sense God's loving presence enfolding the world and us and all that surrounds us. . . . Feel God's desire for the world to be healed, to be whole. . . . Now, come back here, to this room, this time. . . . Feel God's loving concern for you to be whole. . . . Feel God's concern for the persons next to you. . . . For each one in the room. . . . Feel your compassion rising within you, being renewed, strengthened. . . . Let the love of Christ fill you, . . . and realize that this is what you can offer our world. . . . Give thanks for God's work within you and in the world. . . . When you are ready, open your eyes.

To close this prayer time, read aloud these words of hope:

**The risen, living Christ
Calls us by our name;
Comes to the loneliness within us;
Heals that which is wounded within us;
Comforts that which grieves within us;
Seeks for that which is lost within us;
Releases us from that which has dominion over us;
Cleanses us of that which does not belong to us;
Renews that which feels drained within us;
Awakens that which is asleep in us;
Names that which is still formless within us;
Empowers that which is newborn within us;
Consecrates and guides that which is strong within us;
Restores us to this world that needs us;
Reaches out in endless love to others through us.
Amen.**

Engaging the Word (lectio divina, 45 minutes)

Use the steps outlined in the section on leading group *lectio* to guide the group through contemplation of **Isaiah 43:14-19** or **Psalm 104:24-33**.

Closing (5 minutes)

Invite group members to name their longings for the world and ask the group to respond to each one by saying, "Lord, in your mercy, make it so."

Sing the spiritual "Down by the Riverside"; sing again "Here I Am, Lord"; or sing another appropriate song to end the session.

Preparing for Session 5

- Complete the daily readings and entry-point responses in the participant's workbook.

- Read the introductions to the books of Job and Psalms.

- Review the process for leading *lectio divina* until you feel comfortable using it; photocopy and mark the passage for the alternate reader.

- Reflect on and be prepared to model for the group a personal experience of God's guidance toward a particular course of action. (One activity in this session asks group members to reflect on how God guides them and asks them to recount such an experience.)

- Prepare materials for the worship center.

The God

Who Speaks

NOTE: All meeting outlines are for 90-minute sessions; if you are using this study in a 45-minute session, you will need to abbreviate or adapt the opening and closing portions and omit the *lectio divina* experience.

Opening (5 minutes)

Light the Christ candle and say, **We light this candle as a reminder that God's word is a light for our path.**

Invite group members to tell about a Bible verse or phrase that often comes to mind to guide them or one that came to them, that they read, or that was quoted to them at a particular time and helped them with a specific issue.

Sing a hymn or chorus such as "Thy Word Is a Lamp"; "Guide Me, O Thou Great Jehovah"; or another song appropriate for the session.

Interacting with the Word (15 minutes)

Form groups of three. Post your selected questions from the list provided on page 24. Give time for review of responses in the participant's workbook before discussion begins. Once again, encourage group members to listen for God in the responses of others in their small group.

Exploring the Word (20 minutes)

This activity builds on the entry point for Job 10:18-22 (day 2).

Invite participants to review the entry point for day 2 and to list three times in their life when they recognized God's reaching out to them. Then ask them to look for commonalities among the times: did all experiences occur with other people? Did they take place in similar settings—church, outdoors, in the midst of daily activities? Were they aware of God's presence at the time or only when looking back?

Ask the group to help you create a list of the ways God reaches out to us. When the list seems complete, ask if the items on the list have brought to mind additional times or ways God has reached into their lives.

Now ask group members to think back to a time when they consider God to have guided them toward a particular course of action. Model this by briefly telling about your experience and then ask group members to talk about their experiences.

Close this time with a brief prayer of thanks for all the ways God comes to us and seeks to guide us.

Engaging the Word (lectio divina, 45 minutes)

Use the steps outlined in the section on leading group *lectio* to guide the group through contemplation of **Ecclesiastes 4:9-13** or **Psalm 63:1-8**.

Closing (5 minutes)

Read aloud Proverbs 3:3-8. Then invite group members to name situations for which they or someone they know needs God's guidance. Allow time for silent prayer. Close by reading James 3:17 aloud and asking for God's wisdom for all these situations.

Sing a chorus or hymn such as "Savior, Like a Shepherd Lead Us" or another song about God's guidance. Remind group members as they leave, that in Luke 11:9-12 Jesus promises that when we ask for help, an answer will come; that when we ask for a fish, God as a loving parent will not give a snake.

Advise participants to wear clothing with a pocket for the next session.

Preparing for Session 6

- Complete the daily readings and entry-point responses in the participant's workbook.

- Read the introductions to the books of Proverbs, Ecclesiastes, and Lamentations.

- Review the process for leading *lectio divina,* and photocopy and mark the passage for the alternate reader.

- Arrange to use the church sanctuary for the group activity in this session.

- Prepare strips of paper as indicated in EXPLORING THE WORD.

- Prepare materials for the worship center.

A God for All

Seasons

NOTE: All meeting outlines are for 90-minute sessions; if you are using this study in a 45-minute session, you will need to abbreviate or adapt the opening and closing portions and omit the *lectio divina* experience.

Opening (5 minutes)

Light the Christ candle and say, **We light this candle to remember that God is with us in all the seasons of life.**

Invite group members to reflect in silence on what "season" they are experiencing in their life right now. Is it spring, a time of new growth and the promise of flowers soon to bloom? Is it summer, a time of fruitfulness and abundance? Autumn, a time of slowing down, of many beautiful colors? Or is it winter, a time of dormancy and rest? Invite them to pray in silence and then end the prayer time with a short prayer of your own.

Sing a hymn such as "Hymn of Promise" or another appropriate song or chorus to set the tone of the session.

Interacting with the Word (15 minutes)

Select questions from the list provided on page 24. As always, post the questions you'll be using so group members can see them. Give time for review of responses in participant's workbook before discussion begins. Once again, encourage group members to listen for God in the responses of others in their small group.

Exploring the Word (20 minutes)

This activity builds on the entry point for Ecclesiastes 3:1-11 (day 3).

The group will use the church sanctuary as a site for pilgrimage. Take the group to the back of the sanctuary and explain this prayer exercise using these words:

This week we read from the book of Ecclesiastes, which reminds us that there are seasons for everything in our lives. Sometimes life is easy, sometimes hard. Sometimes the right decision seems obvious and other times absolutely inscrutable. And sometimes the same event can cause drastically different emotional responses and reactions. Today we will create a small pilgrimage, reflecting on our life in the light of Ecclesiastes 3 and praying for God's guidance in the push and pull of events.

Give each participant five strips of paper and a pen. Tell the group to write one item of each pair of opposites on one end of a paper strip and the other item of the pair on the opposite end of the paper strip:

> keep/throw away
>
> mourn/dance
>
> be born/die
>
> keep silent/speak
>
> seek/lose

With everyone standing at the back of the sanctuary, say:

Consider these pews (or rows of chairs) your pilgrimage road, your own prayer path. Wander down and back, in and among the pews, making your way to the altar. As you walk, pray about the decisions you have to make, issues that worry you, or a relationship in your life. At each turn in your journey, take out one of your pieces of paper. Consider which opposite word best describes your feelings and thoughts about a situation you are facing. Tear the strip of paper in half and hold the strip that represents your feelings. Put the other part of the strip in your pocket. When you get to the altar, take the strips from

your pocket and leave them there. Take the strips that describe your journey right now and pray for discernment and direction. When you finish praying, make your way back to the meeting room. (Leaders will gather the strips from the altar after the session.)

Engaging the Word (lectio divina, 45 minutes)

Use the steps outlined in the section on leading group *lectio* to guide the group through contemplation of **Proverbs 3:3-8**.

Closing (5 minutes)

Read aloud Ecclesiastes 4:9-12, and invite group members to name people they know who need help and support right now. Begin a prayer asking for God's presence with those persons. Then invite group members to name those who have stood with them in times when they needed help. Offer a prayer of thanksgiving for all those who have been God's presence for us, who have offered us warmth when the world seemed cold.

Sing again "Hymn of Promise" or another appropriate song to end the session.

Preparing for Session 7

- Complete the daily readings and entry-point responses in the participant's workbook.

- Read the introductions to the books of Isaiah and Jeremiah.

- Read an introduction to the major prophets from a study Bible or Bible dictionary.

- Review the process for leading *lectio divina,* and photocopy and mark the passage for the alternate reader.

- Bring for the group exercise:

    1. a copy of local- and international-news sections of a newspaper for each small group

    2. a one-page summary of your church budget showing your congregation's spending in broad categories: building maintenance and utilities, local mission and community outreach programs, international missions, children's ministry, youth ministry, and so on (one copy per person).

    3. a list of names of community and local ministries that members of your congregation are involved in (one copy per person).

- Prepare materials for the worship center.

The Promise of

Restoration

NOTE: All meeting outlines are for 90-minute sessions; if you are using this study in a 45-minute session, you will need to abbreviate and adapt the opening and closing prayers and omit the *lectio divina* experience.

Opening (5 minutes)

Light the Christ candle and say, **We light this candle to remember that God calls us to be holy, to shine as lights in the world.**

Sing a hymn or chorus such as "Change My Heart, O God" or another song appropriate to the session.

Interacting with the Word (15 minutes)

Select questions from the list provided on page 24. Post the questions for all to see. Give time for review of responses in participant's workbook before discussion begins. Once again, encourage group members to listen for God in the responses of others in their small group.

Exploring the Word (20 minutes)

This activity builds on the entry point for Isaiah 58:1-12 (day 3).

Read Isaiah 58:6-12 aloud. Distribute the newspapers and have group members look for examples of "the bonds of injustice," the oppressed, the hungry, the imprisoned, the homeless, and other categories of the suffering and mistreated mentioned in the Isaiah passage. List these on newsprint or a board.

Distribute the copies of the budget and the list of ministries supported by your congregation. Ask group members to match your church's spending and ministries to the categories on the list. Where is your congregation keeping the fast that God chooses? Where do you need to do more?

Invite group members to look at their personal spending and ministry in a similar way in the coming week and to consider literally fasting from food or entertainment and using the money or time they gain to help alleviate suffering.

Engaging the Word (lectio divina, 45 minutes)

Use the steps outlined in the section on leading group *lectio* to guide the group through contemplation of **Jeremiah 29:4-7**.

Closing (5 minutes)

Read aloud Isaiah 58:12 and ask group members to name places where they see God's people rebuilding and restoring.

Close by singing a chorus or hymn about God's power to restore.

Preparing for Session 8

- Complete the daily readings and entry-point responses in the participant's workbook.

- Read the introductions to the books of Ezekiel, Daniel, Hosea, Joel, Amos, Obadiah, Jonah, Micah, Nahum, Habakkuk, Zephaniah, Haggai, Zechariah, and Malachi.

- Read an introduction to the minor prophets from a study Bible or Bible dictionary.

- Review the process for leading *lectio divina,* and photocopy and mark the passage for the alternate reader.

- Prepare strips of paper with the following scripture references:

Hosea 4:1-10; 14:1-7	Nahum 1:1-15
Joel 1:13-20; 2:12-20	Habakkuk 1:1-13; 3:8-19
Amos 2:4-16; 9:9-15	Zephaniah 1:1-9; 3:1-5, 14-20
Obadiah 1:1-21	Haggai 1:1-8, 2:14-23
Jonah 1:1-3, 11-17; 3:1-10	Zechariah 1:1-17; 8:1-8; 10:6-12
Micah 1:1-4; 2:1-7; 4:1-7	Malachi 1:1-10; 3:16-18; 4

  Bring these in a box or bowl so people may draw strips out for the group activity.

- Prepare a worksheet with three columns or sections, one labeled "the accusations/bad actions," another labeled "God's traits," another labeled "God's response." Make a copy for each group member.

- Prepare materials for the worship center.

Waiting and Working for

Justice

NOTE: All meeting outlines are for 90-minute sessions; if you are using this study in a 45-minute session, you will need to abbreviate or adapt the opening and closing portions and omit the *lectio divina* experience.

Opening (5 minutes)

Light the Christ candle and say, **We light this candle in gratitude for the light we have shared over the weeks of this study.**

Invite group members to name ways they have seen evidence of God's steadfast love in the past week.

Sing a hymn such as "Great Is Thy Faithfulness," a chorus, or another song appropriate to the session.

Interacting with the Word (15 minutes)

Select questions from the list provided on page 24. As usual, post the questions for all to see. Give time for review of responses in the participant's workbook before discussion begins. Once again, encourage group members to listen for God in the responses of others in their small group.

Exploring the Word (20 minutes)

This activity will build on the entry point for Habakkuk 2:1-3 (day 5).

Explain that the group is going to look at verses from many if not all of the minor prophets to see how they picture God and God's people. There are twelve strips of paper, each with references to verses from one of the prophets. Form smaller groups of two or three. Decide how you will approach this exercise, having each small group look at more than one book or eliminating some of the prophets, and have someone from each group draw the appropriate number of slips for the assignment. (If you choose to look at fewer prophets' words, consider eliminating Obadiah, Jonah, Nahum, Habakkuk, or Haggai.)

Instruct the groups to read the verses indicated and to fill out the worksheet by listing the charges the prophets make against the people, the traits of God revealed in the passage, and the responses God makes.

Have the small groups report back to the larger group what they found out about each of the prophets. When this is done, ask the group to think about this question: **What have you heard about God's faithfulness that encourages you for the times when you wait to hear from God?** Allow group members to respond as time allows.

Engaging the Word (lectio divina, 40 minutes)

Use the steps outlined in the section on leading group *lectio* to guide the group through contemplation of **Joel 2:21-24**.

Closing (10 minutes)

Silently consider the gifts of these weeks of reading and reflection. Ask group members to name these gifts aloud, and invite the group to respond, "For this gift, O God, we give you thanks."

When all who wish to speak have had an opportunity, pray a closing prayer, giving thanks for the efforts, insights, and participation during the study and asking for continued eagerness to study the Bible.

Sing a closing hymn or chorus such as "Thy Word Is a Lamp" or another that offers thanks for God's message given in the Bible, or allow a group member to suggest a favorite.

Books of

Hebrew Scripture

Created for Relationship

The record of Genesis is fascinating reading, for it is real, even harsh and cruel, yet often piercingly joyful. ***In its pages we find people not unlike ourselves***, whose lives are always under God's watchful eye. Like us, these people are creatures formed by God's hand and inspirited with the very breath of God. Astonishingly, they are transformed even in the midst of their struggles; they deepen in their capacity to respond to God's care.

As you read Genesis slowly and prayerfully, seek to enter into the events described. ***Step into the "shoes" of the people you meet and ask how their situations might apply to your own life.*** Each reading is a new opportunity for God to speak to us through the Holy Spirit and for you to marvel at the ways God loved and formed Abraham and Sarah; Isaac and Rebekah; Jacob, Leah and Rachel.

Key Verse: "I am God Almighty; walk before me, and be blameless. . . . I will establish my covenant between me and you, and your offspring after you throughout their generations, for an everlasting covenant, to be God to you and to your offspring after you" (Genesis 17:1, 7).

Journey from Bondage to Liberation

Among all the books of the canon, *biblical writers quote or refer to Exodus more often than any other book.* Though numerically second in the vast collection of the Hebrew scripture, it has played a foundational role in the development of both Hebrew and Christian traditions. The earliest Christian writers carefully probed this book as they gave expression to the message and meaning of the life of Jesus.

Exodus abounds with themes of profound relevance to the Christian life. As you prayerfully read this book, *give special attention to the symbols and images (such as the sacrificial lamb) that resurface in the Gospels.* Try to identify with the people of Israel as they experience God's hand in their corporate life. Be alert especially to these events and images: the giving of the manna or bread of life, the guiding presence of fire and cloud, the centrality of the tabernacle and tent, and the mountain as a meeting place with God.

Don't read Exodus as a spectator! Watch for opportunities to put yourself in the story, to interact with the narrative. In what ways can you identify with Moses? His self-doubt? His hesitancy to answer God's call to take responsibility for others? His frustration? Or, as you follow Moses up the mountain to converse with God as one "speaks to a friend" (Exod. 33:11), do you find yourself hungering for intimacy with God? The Exodus story is ultimately the story of all God's people from age to age, and it can become our story too.

Key Verse: Then the Lord said, "I have observed the misery of my people who are in Egypt; I have heard their cry on account of their taskmasters. Indeed, I know their sufferings" (Exodus 3:7).

For the Common Good

For many Christians, Leviticus is perhaps the most difficult book of the Bible from which to draw spiritual guidance. We wonder, *What do all these ancient laws about sacrifice have to do with me, anyhow?* And haven't they all been nullified in the death and resurrection of Jesus?

Yet, if you have ever struggled with working out the complex connections among grace, obedience, repentance, and forgiveness, then Leviticus has a great deal to say. The book of Leviticus demonstrates how the people of Israel, as a nation and as individuals, could maintain a righteous relationship with God and receive the blessings that accompany that relationship.

Leviticus teaches us that the proper response to God's saving grace is to live holy lives, lives that are an imitation of God's holiness. In addition, Leviticus demonstrates that God understood that the ancient Israelites, like all humans, were not perfect and so provided a way for them to atone for their sins. Finally, *Leviticus shows that empty ritual and blind compliance are not true worship.* As Jesus and the prophets so clearly recognized and preached, and as the laws of Leviticus make clear, the most ornate worship services are no substitute for the ultimate requirements of God's instruction, or Torah: "Love the LORD your God with all your heart and with all your soul and with all your strength," and "Love your neighbor as yourself" (Deut. 6:5; Lev. 19:18).

As you read Leviticus, be open to experiencing God's forgiveness even as you seek to live out these great commandments.

Key Verse: "You shall be holy, for I the LORD your God am holy" (Leviticus 19:2).

Wandering in the Desert

The book of Numbers portrays God's people at what may be their worst—ungrateful and inattentive. Traveling toward the Promised Land, they do not seem to make much real progress. *Though they have left Egypt physically, they have not left it behind emotionally and spiritually.* Every time something goes wrong or they become unhappy, they criticize Moses and, by association, God. They complain about the manna and water God miraculously gives them. The Israelites harbor jealousy, fight among themselves, offer "unauthorized fire" before the Lord, intermarry with women God tells them to avoid, and publicly criticize one another. *They appear to learn their lessons—but then turn and make the same mistakes again.* God becomes angry with the people but still loves them and repeatedly forgives them.

In short, the book of Numbers portrays the relationship between imperfect people and the Holy One who loves and guides them in spite of their stubbornness. The Israelites are shown God's glory in unmistakable ways; *when they listen and obey, they move toward the good life* that God offers.

Our journey today, like that of the Israelites—from bondage to what God has promised us—is often anything but a straight line or smooth sailing. *But we journey with a patient and faithful God.* Perhaps the greatest lesson from the book of Numbers is that when we are willing to listen and follow, God is always ready to speak to us and guide us.

Key Verse: The people spoke against God and against Moses, "Why have you brought us up out of Egypt to die in the wilderness? For there is no food and no water, and we detest this miserable food" (Numbers 21:5).

Remember to Remember

Have you ever given a farewell address? Imagine Moses' situation. In the process of transferring the leadership of Israel to Joshua, he delivers this address to prepare God's people to enter the Promised Land. God had performed many miracles during the previous years, but almost everyone who had witnessed God's mighty works had died in the desert. And yet, somehow, *Moses must make known all that God has done, direct the people with various laws and decrees, and show them a vision of the future* that they might experience—depending on whether the people remember their relationship with God or go their own way.

The key theme in Deuteronomy is "remembering to remember." And as the book of Deuteronomy opens, *Moses is obviously intent on embedding the memory of God's faithfulness to Israel into the hearts* of his listeners. Israel is urged to remember the past, their present obligations, and the future that the people might build.

In his classic work Letters and Papers from Prison, the Christian martyr *Dietrich Bonhoeffer called forgetfulness "a great problem of Christian ministry."* In what ways do you think this might be so? As you read this foundational book of the Old Testament, ask God to open your heart to the past, to make you sensitive to God's claim on your life today, and to help you anticipate your vivid future with the Lord of your life. See how your memories and your faith are inextricably entwined as you walk with God.

> **Key Verse:** Acknowledge today and take to heart that the LORD is God in heaven above and on the earth beneath; there is no other. Keep his statutes and his commandments, which I am commanding you today for your own well-being and that of your descendants after you, so that you may long remain in the land that the Lord your God is giving you for all time (Deuteronomy 4:39-40).

Good News of Second Chances

When the book of Joshua opens, Israel is still journeying to the Promised Land. Knowing Israel's history of rebelling, *God gives the people another chance to possess the land promised them.* Under Joshua's leadership (and with God's intervention) they finally cross the Jordan River and take control of Canaan. Though God's goals for them have not changed, entering and possessing the land requires of them renewed courage, perseverance, and faith. The Israelites face a difficult task—to conquer and settle the land. *The good news is that God is with them every step of the way.*

As spiritual pilgrims in quest of our own land of promise, we can be encouraged by this story of renewed faith as the Israelites finally take possession of God's gift. The book of Joshua suggests abundant parallels between conquering a geographic Canaan and a spiritual Canaan. How are we called to exercise courage when facing the enemies of our souls? *What does perseverance in daily spiritual practice look like in our lives?* What do we allow to hinder us from possessing our inheritance? How is God giving us a second chance to renew our relationship with him? How is God giving us opportunity to cover new spiritual ground?

> *Key Verse:* [God said,] "No one shall be able to stand against you all the days of your life. As I was with Moses, so I will be with you; I will not fail you or forsake you" (Joshua 1:5).

God's Imperfect People

Within this study designed to help us listen to God, the book of Judges shows what happens when people listen mostly to themselves. It presents **an account of twelve military heroes who deliver Israel from its oppressors**. Not all of these judges are heroes in every sense—one is an assassin (Ehud), and another is sexually promiscuous (Samson). Yet God has raised them up to guide Israel and, for the most part, the judges are inclined to follow the will of the Lord.

The judges' interest in doing God's will is significant because the Israelites are mostly interested in doing their own will; "all the people did what was right in their own eyes" (17:6; 21:25) because "there was no king in Israel" (17:6; 18:1). **The Israelites lived to please themselves and experienced six times in three centuries this cycle**: apostasy (wandering from God), oppression (domination by other things and other nations), renewal and repentance (returning to God), and deliverance by a dynamic leader (freedom based on God-provided human help).

Key Verse: Whenever the LORD raised up judges for them, the LORD was with the judge, and he delivered them from the hand of their enemies all the days of the judge; for the LORD would be moved to pity by their groaning because of those who persecuted and oppressed them (Judges 2:18).

The Power of Relationships

Set squarely within the daily life of common people, the book of Ruth tells a story about people who need God and how God responds. The story demonstrates that, *though mysterious and unpredictable, God's provision can be sought confidently* in the midst of ordinary human problems. The enduring power of the story of Ruth and Naomi rests on the fact that two outcast women—one a foreigner and one an elderly widow—become significant links in the family line of the Christ. God's grace often comes in surprising ways.

This story also reminds us that *God uses people from unexpected places in unexpected ways.* Ruth is not a Hebrew; she cannot inherit a claim to the promises of God to Israel, yet God blesses her with compassion, resourcefulness, and courage. Her faith and love transform a tragic situation into a joyous one.

Redemption—rescuing and reclaiming one apart or adrift—is the central theme of the book of Ruth. The focus is on the management of the land and family obligations, but the story teaches us a more profound meaning of redemption: *God gives new life in abundance where only death and emptiness are expected.* And while God is easing Naomi's and Ruth's need, God is also fulfilling purposes for the whole nation.

Ask yourself where you least expect to find God at work, and give new attention to that place or those people. If you feel like an "outcast," ask what God might be seeking from you and be willing to allow transformation. *Expect to be surprised!*

Key Verse: "Where you go, I will go; where you lodge, I will lodge; your people shall be my people, and your God my God" (Ruth 1:16).

Learning to Listen

The book of First Samuel unfolds like a historical novel, interweaving the lives of the prophet Samuel, King Saul and his family, and David, the God-appointed heir to the throne of Israel. *The nation of Israel is struggling to remain loyal to God as its only supreme ruler* and still survive among surrounding nations that boast superior technology, military organization, and government. Israel, by contrast, relies on a loose tribal confederacy rooted in ancient, sacred law and a faith in God's intervention to save.

We can profitably approach the book of First Samuel by praying the words of one of its early characters: "Speak, Lord, for your servant is listening." Just as the boy Samuel learned early in life to listen deeply (3:1-10), so can we. We can hear God's voice in this story telling us of God's own character and action among humans. We can hear about our own struggles; we too are sometimes pulled between obedient loyalty to God and the temptation to put our trust in self-chosen causes, ideas, and preferences. *We can listen for what it means to be a person after God's own heart* and see how God blesses those who listen. We can claim the promise that God directs and changes human lives today as long ago.

Prepare to realize that promise for yourself as you absorb the reflections and responses suggested in each entry point. As you read ancient words about these anointed leaders—the kings and prophets—let them guide you into a deeper relationship with God.

Key Verse: "Speak, Lord, for your servant is listening" (1 Samuel 3:9).

Seduced by Power

In Second Samuel, ***the young King David comes into his own.*** His story is full of power struggles, duplicity, tragedy, and the violence of war. Presented as "the Lord's anointed," David evokes both admiration and dislike. A musician and a soldier, brave and passionate, he dances with joy, sings praises to God and mourns his sons—all with his whole heart. But personal ambition causes David to trample on other people's lives, and his actions illustrate Lord Acton's maxim: "Power tends to corrupt and absolute power corrupts absolutely." David, however, is remarkable in that, having surrounded himself with advisers unafraid to confront his hypocrisy, ***he listens—to them, to his own conscience, and to the God he loves.*** His imperfect life is lived in constant relationship with the Divine One who is the true sovereign and Israel's only security.

The book of Second Samuel can be read quickly as a compelling story or contemplated slowly. We may identify with the Lord's call to mission—a call that is both daunting and inspiring. We may mourn with David at the tragedies involving his children, reflecting on the difficulties and ambiguities of parenting. We may find ourselves pondering the similarities between these ancient characters and events and some of today's public figures and media headlines. But be sure to ***look through the windows of this story into your own soul—in the ways you deal with the temptations inherent in power and influence.*** Like David, stay aware of the real, enduring power that reposes in God and is lived out in the Lord's Anointed, "great David's greater Son."

Key Verse: David then perceived that the LORD had established him king over Israel, and that he had exalted his kingdom for the sake of his people Israel (2 Samuel 5:12).

Making Room for God

The book of First Kings can be read as the history of a nation on a collision course with itself. The harsh judgment of history turns a glaring spotlight on the deeds of its kings. ***The ancient Israelites are learning life's lessons the hard way.*** The people of Israel have sought the counsel of God and the wisdom of the prophets, but they do not heed, hear, or respond to the call to wholeness.

The account in ***First Kings tells a harsh tale of national tragedy and spiritual bankruptcy.*** Ignorance and pride battle with wisdom; greed and lust diminish prosperity. The people call on prophets for counsel, then ignore, persecute, or even kill them. The ancient Israelite kingdom is divided into two rival nations, north and south, because the nation has lost sight of its spiritual source, the Lord God.

As you read First Kings, ***meditate on how the cycle of sin, repentance, and restoration repeats itself.*** Consider how that same cycle occurs in our lives. As you read and study First Kings, look at your life and see where the call to act now for change strikes home.

Disobedience, evil, hatred, racism, and indifference have existed since the earliest days of humankind. Countless others have already endured many of the personal and national struggles we experience today, yet the presence and love of our forgiving God is not new either! At the heart of the story in First Kings is ***the gracious One who promises to be faithful to us in love*** regardless of the chaos we create.

> ***Key Verse***: "As for you, if you will walk before me, as David your father walked, with integrity of heart and uprightness, doing according to all that I have commanded you, and keeping my statutes and my ordinances, then I will establish your royal throne over Israel forever, as I promised your father David, saying, 'There shall not fail you a successor on the throne of Israel'" (1 Kings 9:4-5).

Our Weakness, God's Power

The book of Second Kings continues the saga of the dearth of God-centered leadership among Israel's kings. It describes Israel's downward slide away from God and into idolatry and immorality—an era of kings who do "evil in the sight of the LORD" by imitating the sins of other nations. ***Once a great nation built by David, Israel is now divided and surrounded*** by powerful enemies and teeters on the verge of complete destruction.

Thirty prophets, most notably Elijah and Elisha, sound the alarm using signs, miracles, warnings, and proclamations—to no avail. Both kingdoms continue to turn from God and are ultimately exiled. Is there any word from the Lord in this desperate situation? The book of Second Kings demonstrates all too clearly the fate of those who stubbornly refuse to follow God's commandments. There is hope, however. ***The God of the covenant always offers hope and restoration.*** A remnant is taken to Babylon to be called into new faithfulness and to receive God's blessings.

Consider how some of these destructive patterns may be at work in our own day. ***What unwise choices and destructive actions undermine the health and spirit of the nation?*** How might we be "exiled" from the blessings we enjoy today if we do not face up to our own behavior?

God still needs faithful and courageous people who are willing to proclaim the truth. As you read, search your own heart for how you can be one of God's faithful people today.

> ***Key Verse:*** The LORD warned Israel and Judah by every prophet and every seer, saying, "Turn from your evil ways and keep my commandments and my statutes, in accordance with all the law that I commanded your ancestors and that I sent to you by my servants the prophets." They would not listen but were stubborn, as their ancestors had been, who did not believe in the LORD their God (2 Kings 17:13-14).

The People of God

If you glance through this book, you will notice the large number of names. *Everywhere are long lists of names*: the generations from Adam to Abraham, the many families descended from the twelve sons of Jacob, the officials of David's court, the priests and Levites who served before the Lord. So many people!

Some of the names have biblical stories connected to them. Some we know from other references, but most are no more than names and titles. *Yet each name represents one of God's people.* Each had a unique role to play in the history of Israel. No doubt many would be surprised that anyone remembers them at all today, three thousand years later.

They are remembered because God still has faithful followers who know they are part of a long tradition. God's people still tell the old, old stories. As people of God—the church—we continue to worship God with prayer, song, musical instruments, and dance. We continue to organize and take on special responsibilities to deal with practical matters. We continue to struggle to know how to be faithful in a confusing and often hostile world.

As you read this book, consider your place among God's people. *How are you tied into the tradition through your family and your church?* What is your special role within your church or within the church as a whole? To what deeper involvement is God calling you?

> *Key Verse:* So all the elders of Israel came to the king at Hebron, and David made a covenant with them at Hebron before the LORD. And they anointed David king over Israel, according to the word of the LORD by Samuel (1 Chronicles 11:3).

Covenants Broken, Covenants Renewed

Covenant is one of the key concepts in the Old Testament. *A covenant is a binding agreement, a promise to behave in a particular way* toward another person or group. God makes covenants with Noah (Genesis 9), Abraham (Genesis 15), the Israelites (Exodus 19–24) and David (2 Samuel 7). The prophets call the people to return to covenant faithfulness while reminding them that God is always faithful— "gracious and merciful, slow to anger, and abounding in steadfast love" (Joel 2:13). Jeremiah looks to a new day when God's covenant will be written directly on our hearts (Jeremiah 31:31-34).

In this second part of the chronicler's account, references to covenant are myriad. Bad kings break the covenant or fail to keep it. Good kings keep the covenant with God. *Great kings are reformers who restore the covenant*, especially Hezekiah (chapters 29–32) and Josiah (chapters 34–35). No other measure—not peace at home or victory in battle—can measure a king's true worth.

In our baptism, God seals the amazing promise to be forever our gracious and forgiving God. God calls us to put our trust in Christ and to respond in obedience. We renew this covenant in many ways throughout our lives: when we take part in the baptism of another, in confirmation and other special services of baptismal renewal, and when we gather at the Lord's table. As you read Second Chronicles, seek to renew your own covenant with your sovereign and loving God.

Key Verse: The king stood in his place and made a covenant before the Lord, to follow the Lord, keeping his commandments, his decrees, and his statutes, with all his heart and all his soul, to perform the words of the covenant that were written in this book (2 Chronicles 34:31).

Ezra

Rebuilding and Reclaiming

There are plenty of instances in history where a nation was exiled and never received its homeland back. Think, for example, of the Armenians, who have suffered massacres and who are without their ancient land; and think of the Kurdish people, now spread out in Turkey, Iraq, and elsewhere. Yet, against all odds, ***God restored the people of Israel to Jerusalem and made provision for rebuilding the Temple.*** Of course, Israel was not just any nation exiled, and the Temple was not just any temple destroyed. This nation was the chosen of the one, true God. They had worshiped God in the Temple that lay in ruins: "By the rivers of Babylon—there we sat down and there we wept when we remembered Zion" (Ps. 137:1).

Beneath the rather dry lists and the copies of official documents and decrees in the book of Ezra, this is a dramatic story—a resurrection story. ***What seems like the death of a nation is, in reality, new life.*** Have you ever been forced to live away from home for an extended period of time? Do you know people who are refugees from their homes? Try to place yourself in this story. Imagine the emotions God's people experience as they return to their ancient land: "The wonder of it! We never expected this! Is it too good to be true? How could we have imagined that God would forget the covenant, that God would no longer be gracious and loving toward us?" ***While Israel may be faithless, God is forever faithful!***

> **Key Verse:** With joy they celebrated the festival of unleavened bread seven days; for the LORD had made them joyful, and had turned the heart of the king of Assyria to them, so that he aided them in the work on the house of God, the God of Israel (Ezra 6:22)

Remember Who You Are

The task that Nehemiah and his people faced was formidable. With limited resources and in the midst of political pressure and sabotage, they began to rebuild the walls of their beloved city Jerusalem. Under the guidance of Nehemiah, they had reconstructed the temple, but the challenges of rebuilding had demoralized them. In this book, *we see how Nehemiah's reliance on and faith in God helped him lead his people to accomplish a task successfully*, restore their courage, and renew their respect and appreciation for God's Word. Nehemiah, a man of action, was also a man of deep faith. Because he lived in relationship with the all-knowing God, he knew when to pray and when to act.

In the book of Nehemiah, we find more than an historical account of God's people at a certain point in time; we discover a reminder that we are partners with God. We are not exiles recently returned to our homeland. Our destroyed city walls do not need to be rebuilt. Yet *we are called just as surely to be builders of faithful lives, relationships, and communities.* If you face these tasks with feelings of being overwhelmed or inadequate, you'll be able to identify with Nehemiah. Just as surely as he struggled with issues of motivation, fatigue, and criticism, so too do we today. But this book also offers inspiration to lean on the living God as we go about our building tasks.

> *Key Verse:* Then I said to them, "You see the trouble we are in, how Jerusalem lies in ruins with its gates burned. Come, let us rebuild the wall of Jerusalem, so that we may no longer suffer disgrace." I told them that the hand of my God had been gracious upon me, and also the words that the king had spoken to me. Then they said, "Let us start building!" So they committed themselves to the common good (Nehemiah 2:17-18).

When Bad Things Happen

Read the book of Job as a drama being played out on a stage. Act I begins with Job living in happiness and prosperity. Then, through one calamity after another, Job loses everything—his livestock, his servants, his children, his health. In Act II Job converses with his friends, who try to help him make sense of his suffering. In Act III *Job speaks directly with God, and Job grasps—apparently for the first time—the depth of God's power and love.* Job knows he has personally encountered the eternal God: "I had heard of you by the hearing of the ear, but now my eye sees you" (42:5).

The book of Job endures as a drama because it addresses the reality of suffering. Not surprisingly, Job struggles more with the crisis of faith going on within him than he does with what has happened to him externally. But *Job persists in loving God*—refusing to curse God—in spite of all his deeply felt losses. He never abandons his own honest, relentless, and tormented pursuit of God.

All of us eventually travel the way of suffering. As we journey into its darkness, we may find ourselves tempted to doubt God's goodness, mercy, and love. But *Job gives us the courage to face honestly our hard questions and to wrestle with God.* Like Job, we may meet God face-to-face at a depth we have not known before. Like Job, we can come to know that when all we have is taken away, God is enough.

Key Verse: "I had heard of you by the hearing of the ear, but now my eye sees you" (Job 42:5).

Honest to God

The life of prayer, like life itself, is not always happy and peaceful. Into prayer we take our anxieties, loneliness, and discouragement along with our joy, awe, and celebration. *In order to deepen any intimate relationship, we must be honest about our feelings.* Relating to the God of the universe is no different. In fact, God knows us better than we know ourselves and always desires "truth in the inward being" (Ps. 51:6).

The book of Psalms demonstrates such honest prayer. It contains songs of praise and prayers of lament, hymns celebrating God's steadfast love, and prayers for vindication against enemies. The psalmists recall God's faithful love and extol the marvels of the created order. As we read, we share the psalmists' loneliness, sickness, grief, and dread. We experience with them the ups and downs of their genuine spiritual journeys.

Perhaps no other book in the Bible has been read and meditated on as much as the book of Psalms. In most monasteries, the Psalms are recited from morning until night. Through prayerful repetition, the Psalms reach deeper and deeper into our hearts. *When we "pray the psalms," we find new dimensions in our relationship with God.* The Psalms are a sanctuary of prayer to which we may daily retreat and find crucial nourishment for our hearts.

Key Verse: Your word is a lamp to my feet
and a light to my path (Psalm 119:105).

Wisdom Day by Day

Proverbs is perhaps the most practical book in the Bible. These words of wisdom grew out of the common experiences of human life. The teachers of ancient times were eager to share what they had learned about life. Their insights helped them in their daily living and relationships. *The reward of wisdom is a better and happier life.* Thus, this "treasure" is more precious than silver or gold and worthy of passing on. The sayings here cover a variety of themes: love, friendship, marriage, poverty, wealth, and others.

Individual proverbs summarize wisdom that has proved true in varied situations. But they are not absolute or applicable in every circumstance. If not taken in proper context, some may even contradict each other: "Too many cooks spoil the broth," but "Many hands make light work." *True wisdom is not simply knowing the sayings of the wise but also knowing when and how to apply them.*

Some proverbs may trouble us. The question of why evil besets innocent people, for example, may continue to baffle and disturb us as we meditate on some adages in this book. Nevertheless, the wisdom we find here can help us walk in the Spirit in the midst of our doubts and all that life offers—good or bad. *Remember that getting insight does not mean finding quick answers.* As you read and ponder, allow your soul, heart, and mind to wrestle with the sages and, like Jacob wrestling with an angel, to hold on until you receive a blessing.

> *Key Verse:* Wisdom is supreme; therefore get wisdom. Though it cost all you have, get understanding (Proverbs 4:7).

A Search for Meaning

Ecclesiastes explores the meaning of life, and its words often seem to reflect Thoreau's famous quotation, "The mass of men [and women] lead lives of quiet desperation." The author, called "the Teacher," is not as conclusive in his exploration as we would like him to be; at times he seems uncertain about God's ways. We might wonder why he sends all of these mixed messages. He confesses that his past choices have included the pursuit of pleasure, achievement, and riches (2:1-11; 4:13-16; 5:1–6:12). Even though the Teacher has found all three, he struggles with disillusionment. In contrast, his parting words seem sure of the purpose of life: "Fear God, and keep his commandments; *for that is the whole duty of everyone." We identify with the struggle to find meaning in the weariness of everyday life*, a universal struggle to this day; yet beyond the recitation of troubles, the words soar with hope : "[God] has made everything suitable for its time" (3:11).

As you read this book of wisdom, *take time to ponder the "big picture"— the meaning and purpose of life*—but don't forget to make a daily effort to look with wonder at God's creation and remember that it is "beautiful in its time" (niv). Learn from the Teacher about the meaninglessness of acquisition, knowledge, and work in and of themselves—but also learn that our ultimate purpose in everything we do is to know, love, and serve God. Even as you acknowledge the ambiguities of life, *remain open to the rich and mysterious ways in which God will reveal its meaning to you*.

> *Key Verse:* [God] has made everything suitable for its time; moreover he has put a sense of past and future into their minds, yet they cannot find out what God has done from the beginning to the end (Ecclesiastes 3:11).

Afflicted and Comforted

Although many biblical books contain poignant expressions of grief in poetry and song, Lamentations is the only book in Hebrew scripture composed solely of such expressions. The author grieves over the destruction of Jerusalem, the Hebrew people's infidelity to God, and the punishment that comes at the hands of the Babylonians when the chosen people turned from God.

Like the author of Lamentations, we can turn to God in times of anguish and pain. *We can pour out our sorrow from the depths of our souls as we look for God's healing love.* Turning to God also means taking responsibility for our actions, repenting of misdeeds, and accepting the new life that God offers us. No matter what our personal pain or sorrow, Lamentations tells us, God is the rock to whom we can turn. Whatever our afflictions, God's loving arms reach out to comfort us.

Key Verse: The steadfast love of the LORD never ceases,
his mercies never come to an end (Lamentations 3:22).

Faithful Response to God's Glory

The prophet Isaiah has a message for God's people who are "defying his glorious presence" (3:8). *Isaiah is called (6:9-10) to confront the people with the dire consequences of their rebellion* against their God who nonetheless remains faithful to them.

Chapters 1–39 are dominated by dark and vivid pictures of the devastation that human beings invite by defying the Lord's presence and purposes. When they stubbornly refuse to respect the fabric of creation, they experience the power of God in creation as a terror. When they do not live in the holiness that God calls them to, they ultimately experience God's holiness as wrath and judgment. *The people are challenged to purify themselves and give up their persistent reliance on ritual magic and political maneuvering.*

Such purifying change opens God's people to the Spirit's illumination of new insight into God's loving design for Israel. Chapters 40–66 overflow with promises of divine comfort, and restoration. In the new era, *the Israelites are called to be a servant people who will cooperate with God's purposes for the whole of humanity*—purposes greater than any they could imagine.

We glimpse, through Isaiah's poetry, some very specific social situations and highly personal emotions that God's people experience. As you read, be alert to parallels in your own life. *Pay attention to how God may be working in you—judging, purifying, and filling you with a wider vision* of the "glorious presence." Consider how God is calling you to cooperate with redeeming love in the world.

> *Key Verse:* "Holy, holy, holy is the LORD of hosts;
> the whole earth is full of his glory" (Isaiah 6:3).

Hope in Times of Weeping

"Who am I called to be?" ***"How does God intend to use my gifts?"***
Jeremiah wrestles with such questions and finds that God has rich
purposes for his life. Jeremiah the prophet is a passionate man who
grieves with God for a wayward people.

Jeremiah the proclaimer of God's word is a person of enormous
courage—speaking at great personal cost in a climate of hostility and
rejection. Jeremiah the poet is a person of such transparency of soul
that he hears God and weeps with God. Jeremiah declares to listeners
that God is a father who wants good things for us, such as "a desirable
land, the most beautiful heritage of all the nations" (3:19); God so
deeply loves "my dear son . . . the child I delight in" (31:20), that
even though we reject and deny the call, God continues to show
mercy. Jeremiah the servant of God is ***a man of great integrity who calls
the people of God to integrity*** so that they might not lose their true
identity as God's children.

From the perspective of the sixth century B.C., ***Jeremiah shows us a God
who yearns for us, a God who has wonderful things in store for us, a God
who grieves when we turn away.*** Jeremiah calls us to repent and to
grieve when we fail to respond to a love that passionately desires our
good. And as we respond, we discover the compassion of God, who
alone can restore us.

Key Verse: "Is Ephraim my dear son?
　　　　Is he the child I delight in?
　　As often as I speak against him,
　　　　I still remember him.
　　Therefore I am deeply moved for him;
　　　　I will surely have mercy on him,
　　says the LORD (Jeremiah 31:20).

Confronting the Holy

Many people know this book primarily by **the author's vision of a valley of dry bones.** But in these pages we also meet a priest and prophet who agonizes over the poor choices of the leaders of Israel, who bemoans the sins of the people, and who condemns the desecration performed by neighboring nations.

With words and images that seem abrasive at times, yet always penetrating, Ezekiel invites us to look to the One whom we worship. He calls us to worship God with authenticity (14:6). Through his account we meet a God who is angry and disappointed (9:9-10), a God who laments the disasters that will come upon unjust nations (30:1-4), and a God who cares for people as a shepherd cares for a flock of sheep (34:1-24). **This God holds people accountable for their actions (23:35), desires to make a new covenant of peace (34:25), and longs to put a new heart and a new spirit in them (36:26).** Renewal will flow like a river to all the land (47:1).

Woven throughout the book of Ezekiel is the refrain, "Then they shall know that I am the LORD." **As we read Ezekiel, we find ourselves confronted and challenged, loved and renewed,** and ready to sing the refrain, "Now I know that you are the LORD my God." Pray for openness to hear the words of Ezekiel and a soft heart with which to accompany him into God's presence.

Key Verse: "Then the nations that are left all around you shall know that I, the LORD, have rebuilt the ruined places, and replanted that which was desolate; I, the LORD, have spoken, and I will do it" (Ezekiel 36:36).

The Power to Stand

The book of Daniel is a story of intrigue and mystery, of dreams and visions and miracles. It is also the story of four *young men who find the power to stand firm while living in a culture whose values oppose their faith.*

Daniel, Hananiah, Mishael, and Azariah are carried away as captives to Babylon when Jerusalem falls. They are of royal and noble lineage—four of the finest young men of Judah—and so they are chosen for special roles. They are given new names (Belteshazzar, Shadrach, Meshach, and Abednego) and are to be educated and groomed for service in Nebuchadnezzar's court, learning the literature, language, and customs of Babylon.

Shadrach, Meshach, and Abednego refuse to worship the image the king has set up. The advisers to the Babylonian king oppose the young men for expressing their faith, and they plot against them. *The young men, however, pray for one another and stand together.* Daniel rises to a place of power in the kingdom as an interpreter of the king's dreams, and he writes down his visions of how God will work in human events.

The book of Daniel shows how *the faithful can triumph even in difficult situations by remaining true to God* and living by God's standards despite opposition from the culture. Their reliance on one another and on the power of prayer are models that all of us can use as a pattern for our lives, whatever the difficult situations in which we find ourselves.

> *Key Verse:* "We will not serve your gods and we will not worship the golden statue that you have set up" (Daniel 3:18).

Unwavering Love

In the book of Hosea, *God calls, confronts, and woos the people of Israel.*
Herein unfolds the account of a rebellious Israel—a people looking
to idols rather than to God. God directs the prophet Hosea to marry
Gomer, a prostitute, to be a living metaphor of God's unwavering
love to the unfaithful people. Hosea marries Gomer, knowing she will
be repeatedly unfaithful. God instructs Hosea to remain faithful
regardless of Gomer's behavior. Hosea obeys (3:1-2), and, while the
people deserve God's wrath, through the drama of his life Hosea
demonstrates God's constant love for Israel.

The Israelites vacillate between clinging to idol worship and crying
out to God for help. Israel's sin is so great that the people become "as
vile as the thing they [love]" (9:10). Yet *in a dramatic flood of
compassion, God acts*—not as a human being would, but as only God
can (11:8-11), choosing to forgive the people and draw them near
once again.

This book has much to say about *the human propensity to look anywhere
but to God for meaning and comfort.* Even more vividly, it reminds us of
the wonder of God's faithful love to persistently unfaithful people.
Why does God repeatedly forgive and love a people who deserve only
judgment? As passionately as anywhere in scripture, the book of
Hosea speaks of God's intention to be Israel's faithful, loving spouse.
As you read Hosea, *let God nurture in you an intimate relationship that is
the fruit of knowing and receiving God "in spirit and in truth"* (John 4:24).

Key Verse: Return, O Israel, to the LORD your God (Hosea 14:1).

The Coming Day of the Lord

Is "the day of the LORD" a day of judgment or a day of salvation? Is it a day of wrath or a day of restoration? As we read Joel's prophecy, we discover that it is both. God's earlier judgment against the apostasy of Judah is reversed not by the actions of the people but by God's loving determination to restore the people to fellowship and life. ***This prophecy is a debate within the very mind of God***—the people of Judah deserve judgment (a plague of locusts) and yet ***God wants to offer miraculous mercy*** (the gift of abundant life).

God waits for each of us to rend our hearts, to repent and to receive in faith the salvation that God desires to give us. ***Through the prophet Joel, God invites us to listen.*** You will be standing on holy ground as you read, for the message of the book of Joel is that God's arms are extended to you, inviting you to return so that you may stand in God's presence in "the day of the LORD"—a day when God's Spirit would be poured out on all people.

Key Verses: Then afterward
   I will pour out my spirit on all flesh;
     your sons and your daughters shall prophesy,
   your old men shall dream dreams,
     and your young men shall see visions.
   Even on the male and female slaves,
     in those days, I will pour out my spirit.
Then everyone who calls on the name of the LORD shall be saved; for in Mount Zion and in Jerusalem there shall be those who escape, as the LORD has said, and among the survivors shall be those whom the LORD calls (Joel 2:28-29, 32).

Let Justice Roll Down

Perhaps **nowhere in the Bible is God's desire for justice and righteousness more explicitly proclaimed than in the book of Amos.** Again and again, Amos details the sins of a society that thinks it has it all together—it is prospering economically and militarily as it proclaims faith in the one true God. But Amos peers beneath the prosperous and religious surface, and what he sees spells doom for Israel.

The name Amos means "burden bearer," and this prophet bears the burden of speaking painful truths to errant Israel. Amos, not a prophet by trade, is a herdsman and cultivator of sycamore trees. This outdoorsman-tradesman declares the word of the Lord in terms familiar to him: vineyards and trees, marketplaces and caravan customs.

Amos is not an easy or comforting book to read, but its words are as relevant today as they were almost three thousand years ago. We cannot get around the book's hard-hitting truth: If we misuse power or have gained wealth unjustly, **if we are indifferent to the suffering of the distressed and disadvantaged, we are to stop and "seek the LORD and live."** As you read this book, try to see ways in which you resemble the people of Israel, no matter how disturbing it may be to do so.

Like any good prophet, **Amos offers hope as well as reproach.** There is no mistaking the kind of life God desires for us, and that life is an existence far more meaningful and fulfilling than any we could ever imagine in the midst of our comfortable complacency.

> **Key Verse:** Let justice roll down like waters,
> and righteousness like an ever-flowing stream (Amos 5:24).

God's Passion for Justice

No one likes to be treated unfairly or to see others so treated. When injustices occur, *it helps to know that God is watching and will see that justice ultimately prevails.*

Although the book of Obadiah gives us very little information about the prophet, it reiterates God's zeal for justice, a theme that is woven throughout the prophetic books. Therefore God pledges to bring judgment on the people of Edom, who stand by (and even cause harm) while their Israelite kinfolk are conquered (v. 11). Obadiah declares that God will bring "the day of the LORD," a day of judgment for all the nations (vv.15–16). *God will not forget those who are treated unfairly!*

In these twenty-one verses we are once again impressed with God's passion for justice. And *we know that in the end all nations and people—indeed, all of life—belong to God.* "And the kingdom shall be the LORD's" (v. 21).

Key Verse: For the day of the LORD is near against all the nations.
As you have done, it shall be done to you;
your deeds shall return on your own head (Obadiah 15).

Running from God

At first glance the book of Jonah is an account of the strangest two-way journey ever described: A reluctant prophet flees in fear as far away as ships could sail, only to return to land within the belly of a giant fish. But the story of Jonah's strange journey underlines a great truth: ***God can use even a stubborn and reluctant prophet to bring the truth to those who need to hear it.*** In spite of Jonah's ungracious willfulness, God's compassion prevails—the entire population of Nineveh repents and experiences God's healing love.

This fascinating story makes us wonder if Jonah ever clearly grasped that *"the love of God is broader than the measure of our mind,"* as an old hymn says. God's compassion is so great and unwavering that we, like Jonah, struggle to believe it. We wince at the prospect of having to imitate it, particularly when we need to demonstrate it to certain people.

As you read this book, you may identify with Jonah's struggle as he first does the wrong thing and then finally does the right thing but with a wrong heart. Perhaps you have felt at odds with what God has asked you to do, and so you've offered a stiff handshake or a fake smile. ***You've kept at a distance people whom God would have you love.*** Let God penetrate the areas of your life in which you barely cooperate or even resist. Experience God's wonderfully embracing love for you—and for others—even when you feel tempted to run.

Key Verse: "Should I not be concerned about Nineveh, that great city?" (Jonah 4:11).

What God Requires

Micah looks beneath the surface of Judah's society and sees fundamental flaws that will result in the nation's downfall. Greed and dishonesty permeate the nation, and the result is a compromised legal system, a callous disregard for the poor, and an unethical business practice. Ironically, all this takes place while Judah publicly professes to be faithful to the one true God and to the divine law handed down to the people during their desert wandering. *They are hypocrites; their religion is a sham, and God is angry.*

Micah's prophetic words give us occasion to ask ourselves several questions: *How can I be willing to hear all that God has to say, even when it is unpleasant?* How might God be speaking to me about my thoughts and activities in light of the faith I profess? How do I need to participate in calling society to account for being less than it professes to be? How can I claim for myself Micah's hope for a time when a just and peaceful world will be God's prized possession? *How open am I to acknowledging God's presence in every area of my life?*

Key Verse: He has told you, O mortal, what is good;
  and what does the LORD require of you
but to do justice and to love kindness,
and to walk humbly with your God? (Micah 6:8).

Woe and Reassurance

The prophet Nahum is given a vision, and with poetic passion he tells the world what he sees. *His call is to announce that God opposes the arrogant Assyrian empire* and will bring about the downfall of Nineveh, the proud city of Assyria. Nahum's descriptions are astonishingly powerful:

> Ah! City of bloodshed,
>   utterly deceitful, full of booty—no end to the plunder!
> The crack of whip and rumble of wheel,
>   galloping horse and bounding chariot!
> Horsemen charging, flashing sword and glittering spear,
> piles of dead,
>   heaps of corpses,
> dead bodies without end—they stumble over the bodies! (3:1–3).

The language is terse and clear: "There is no assuaging your hurt; your wound is mortal" (3:19).

Among the Israelites, though, there will be rejoicing. The images of destruction also contain a word of hope for the people of Israel, long oppressed by the Assyrians: "Look! On the mountains the feet of one who brings good tidings, who proclaims peace!" (1:15). *Nahum calls us to look at our own arrogance and faithlessness and welcome the herald who brings us news of peace and hope.*

Key Verse: Look! On the mountains the feet of one who brings good tidings, who proclaims peace! Celebrate your festivals, O Judah, fulfill your vows, for never again shall the wicked invade you; they are utterly cut off (Nahum 1:15).

Waiting and Hoping

Habakkuk, a seventh-century B.C. Judean prophet, is pressed between the two horns of a dilemma of faith. On one side are his people, the people of God, living as faithlessly as though they are not God's people at all. On the other side are surrounding nations whose "own might is their god" (1:11), yet who have been given a role in punishing God's errant people. As the pressure mounts Habakkuk cries out to the Lord and encounters silence. *Habakkuk is restless, hungry for answers.* The result is a prophet's narrative of waiting and hoping, hoping and waiting.

Although Habakkuk never receives complete answers to his difficult questions about justice and fairness, *he does receive a word from the Lord that encourages him.* A book that begins in a desperate cry ends with a song declaring that "God, the LORD, is my strength; he makes my feet like the feet of a deer, and makes me tread upon the heights" (3:19). As the prophet waits through trouble, *he has a sure and certain hope that God will save him.*

As you read these three intense chapters, recall times when it seemed to you that life was unfair, that there were more questions than answers or that God was slow to reveal divine purposes. *When have you prayed, "How long . . . ?"* When have you sensed that God was telling you to "wait" for insight or resolution to a problem? Where have you found hope in such times?

Key Verse: There is still a vision for the appointed time;
     it speaks of the end, and does not lie.
If it seems to tarry, wait for it;
     it will surely come, it will not delay (Habakkuk 2:3).

Quieted by God's Love

A day of judgment is coming quickly, says the prophet Zephaniah, when God is going to make a clean sweep of Judah and the nations around it. In these three chapters we learn that the priests, prophets, leaders, and people are involved in idol worship (1:4-5), are complacent in doing justice while accumulating quantities of gold and silver (1:12, 18), and are arrogantly rebelling against God's instructions (3:11). *Yet hope and promise are woven through the predictions of darkness and gloom.*

The humble and righteous will find shelter on the day of trouble and ruin (2:3), and *the lowly and humble will remain as a faithful remnant* (3:12-13). The greatest word of hope comes at the end of Zephaniah in a chorus of praise in which God promises to keep the nation from the impending disaster, to gather all the scattered people and bring them home, and to reestablish the Judeans as a people of honor and blessing (3:14-20).

Though we may have different idols and face different threats, the call of Zephaniah is just as important for us today; it is a call to live a life of humble obedience before God. We are to be aware of what God has done in the past and let that remembrance keep us humbly walking on the right path. *There must always be room in our lives for praise, because God delights in us,* renews us with love, and exults over us with singing.

Key Verse: The LORD, your God, is in your midst,
      a warrior who gives victory;
    he will rejoice over you in gladness,
      he will renew you in his love;
    he will exult over you with loud singing (Zephaniah 3:17).

Examine Your Ways

Haggai encourages his listeners to anticipate that the rebuilding of the temple will set in motion a new chain of events that will reveal God's powerful presence. Haggai, a prophet in the court of King Darius (about 520 b.c.), wants *to inspire the Israelites and capture their imaginations with the vision of a rebuilt Jerusalem*, where God will once again be honored and praised.

Beaten down and focused on survival under alien rule, God's people are in despair. They have returned from exile physically but haven't yet returned "home" to God—they haven't begun to rebuild God's house. They can see failed crops and a government in chaos; *they cannot see hope for their future.*

As you read these two short chapters containing Haggai's oracles, reflect on these questions: *Have you ever felt so oppressed by events in your life that you lost your focus on God?* Do you in some way long for the "good old days" when things were better for you? Are you dissatisfied with the present? Have you given up on God and decided that you have to take care of things yourself? Haggai helps us put life in perspective, for he brings the message that hope in *God is always the best option.*

Key Verses: Then the word of the LORD came through the prophet Haggai: "Is it a time for you your-selves to be living in your paneled houses, while this house remains a ruin?" (Haggai 1:3-4)

Not by Might

Zechariah seems to say, "Let's start over, refocus ourselves on God, and get busy." The task at hand is the rebuilding of the Temple that has lain in ruins since its destruction by the Babylonians. *The focus for the future is on rebuilding the spiritual life of a people* who have endured humiliation and exile. To complicate the problem, the people are apathetic about their task and indifferent to the call to restore their worship to its former glory. But the prophet reminds the returned exiles that they have a golden opportunity to renew their relationship with God—God is waiting to wrap loving arms around this people who had previously snubbed their Creator.

So too *God stands ready to quiet each of us with love* if we earnestly desire to receive that love. In God's strength we can rebuild that which has been broken down. With God's vision we can look toward a future of new possibilities. What is God saying to you about your future? *Are you open to this motivating, energizing, divine love*—love that offers new life in this world and in eternity?

> **Key Verses:** Thus says the LORD of hosts: I will save my people from the east country and from the west country; and I will bring them to live in Jerusalem. They shall be my people and I will be their God, in faithfulness and in righteousness (Zechariah 8:7–8).

Keeping Promises

In the book of Malachi, the prophet's words, not his person, demand our attention. We know next to nothing about the prophet himself, but *we find in his writing a vibrant word from God* (the name of the book means "my messenger").

Malachi, using a question-and-answer device, challenges the people to mend their ways. The prophet warns the priests about offering blemished sacrifices (1:8) and giving false teachings (2:8). He confronts the people about mixed marriages and divorce (2:10-16) and about not paying a full tithe (3:8-10). *The day of judgment is coming, he declares, and it will be like a fire*—it will burn away evil and refine what is good.

Amid Malachi's warnings and judgment, the prophet tells of *wonderful blessings that will belong to those who are faithful and obedient to God.* Those who are generous and bring a full tithe will see God "open the windows of heaven for you and pour down for you an overflowing blessing" (3:10). Those who revere and honor God will see the sun of righteousness "rise, with healing in its wings" (4:2). Malachi calls us to return to a life of honest worship, truthful speech, and generous compassion. *Listen with your heart, respond with your deeds, and the Lord will come to you!*

> ***Key Verse:*** Ever since the days of your ancestors you have turned aside from my statutes and have not kept them. Return to me, and I will return to you, says the Lord of hosts. But you say, "How shall we return?" (Malachi 3:7).

What Is

Spiritual Formation?

HUMAN BEINGS ARE creatures of the future. Unlike other inhabitants of creation whose lives are fixed within the boundaries of genetics and instinct, human existence is open-ended, laced with mystery, like moist clay in a potter's hand. We are works in progress, shaped by the constant rhythms of nature and the unexpected turns of history. Sometimes elated and sometimes burdened by our unfinished condition, we live our days conscious that "what we will be has not yet been made known" (1 John 3:2). A sense of our true identity is always just beyond our grasp, always awaiting us, it seems, just around the next bend in the road.

As nature and history interact with a human existence that is incomplete, pliable and rich with significant potential, personal formation occurs. *Human beings are formed by the sculpting of will, intellect, and emotion into a distinct way of being in the world.* Such formation of personal character will assume a wide range of expression depending on our location geographically, socially, economically and culturally. Family values, social conventions, cultural assumptions, the great turning points of an epoch, the painful secrets of a heart—these and many other factors combine to form or deform the direction, depth and boundaries of our lives. Formation is therefore a fundamental characteristic of human life. It is happening whether or not we are aware of it, and its effect may as often inhibit as promote the development of healthy, fulfilled humanity.

For people of biblical faith, nature and history of themselves are not the final sources of personal formation. Rather, they are means through which the God who formed all things molds human beings into the contours of their truest destiny: the unfettered praise of God (see Isaiah 43:21). To be shaped by God's gracious design is a particular expression of personal formation—spiritual formation. Irenaeus, third-century bishop of Lyons, echoed this ancient biblical theme when he observed that *"the glory of God is the human being fully alive."* The God known in scripture is a God who continuously forms something out of nothing—earth and heaven, creatures great and small, a people who call upon God's name, the "inmost being" (Psalm 139:13) of every human life. Yet the majestic sweep of God's formational activity never eclipses the intimacy God desires and seeks with us. Having carefully and lovingly formed each of us in the womb, God knows us by name and will not forget us (see Isaiah 43:1; 44:21, 24). In the biblical perspective, to be a person means to exist in a relationship of ongoing spiritual formation with the God whose interest in us extends to the very roots of our being.

For Christians, the pattern and fulfillment of God's work of spiritual formation converge in a single figure—Jesus Christ. Jesus is the human being fully alive, fully open to God's work in the world. Simultaneously, Jesus is God's work fully alive, fully embodied in the world. For all who are heavily burdened and wearied by the torments of the world, for all who long to dwell in the house of the Lord, Jesus is the level way, the whole truth and the radiant life. Christians are placed daily before the greatest of all choices: *to be conformed to the luminous image of Jesus Christ* through the gracious assistance of God the Holy Spirit or to be conformed to the ravaged image of the world through the deceitful encouragement of the "powers of this dark world" (Romans 12:2; Ephesians 6:10-13).

Spiritual formation in the Christian tradition, then, is a lifelong process through which our new humanity, hidden with Jesus Christ in God, becomes ever more visible and effective through the leading of the Holy Spirit. *Spiritual formation at its best has been understood to be at once fully divine and fully human—that is, initiated by God and manifest in both vital communities of faith and in the lives of individual disciples.* We see this theme carried through the history of the church, from Paul's introduction of formation in Jesus Christ as the central work of Christian life (Galatians 4:19) to early formational writings such as the Didache (second century); to the formative intent of monastic rules; to the shaping purpose of Protestant manuals of piety; to the affirmation of lay formation in the documents of Vatican II; and finally to the current search for practices that open us to God.

OUR NEW HUMANITY

Our unfinished character leads us to acknowledge that *"what we will be has not yet been made known."* Yet Christians, looking at Jesus Christ, can add with confident hope that "we shall be like him" (1 John 3:2). This hope originates in the hidden dimensions of baptism. Baptism unites us with the full sweep of Jesus' life and death, resurrection, and ascension in glory to the eternal communion of love enjoyed by our triune God. In baptism, motifs of cleansing from the stain of sin coexist with images of death and rebirth to signal the radically new life we enter through this spiritual birth canal (John 3:1–6).

At the center of this rebirth from above is the Paschal mystery—*the pattern of self-relinquishment and loving availability Jesus freely manifested in his ministry and in his final journey* to Jerusalem and Golgotha. This is the mysterious pattern of God's work in the world, the pattern of loss that brings gain, willing sacrifice that yields abundance, self-forgetfulness that creates a space for the remembering God. It is the pattern that steers our course from bondage to freedom—from the ways of the old Adam, who turned and hid from the One who so lovingly formed him, *to the freedom of the new Adam*, Jesus Christ, who lives with God in unbroken intimacy.

This unfolding of baptismal grace in daily life, this passing from bondage to freedom, is spiritual formation. Because *spiritual formation draws us into the fullness of life in Jesus Christ*, it shares the qualities of Jesus Christ. Thus, spiritual formation is eminently personal yet inherently corporate: *It erases nothing of our unique humanity but transposes it into a larger reality*—the mystical body of Jesus Christ in and through which we are, as the Episcopal Book of Common Prayer notes, "very members incorporate" of one another. Spiritual formation is also fully human, reflecting our own decisions, commitments, disciplines and actions. At the same time, *spiritual formation is wholly divine, an activity initiated by God and completed by God*, in which we have been generously embraced for the sake of the world.

THE HOLY SPIRIT'S LEADING

The sweeping movement of grace by which the world was created and is sustained is orchestrated by God the Holy Spirit. In God's sovereign freedom, the Holy Spirit stirs where the Spirit chooses. Remarkably, *the Spirit has selected human life as a privileged place of redemptive activity.* In the day-to-day rhythms of our life, the Holy Spirit comes to us with gentle persistence, inviting us to join the wondrous dance of life with God. In this holy dance the Spirit always takes the lead, a partner both sensitive and sure. *"The spiritual life is the life of God's Spirit in us,"* notes spiritual writer Marjorie Thompson, "the living interaction between our spirit and the Holy Spirit through which we mature into the full stature of Christ and become more surrendered to the work of the Spirit within and around us."

There are settings and disciplines that prepare us to recognize and respond to the Holy Spirit's invitation. The church, the body of Jesus Christ visible and tangible in the world, as rich with promise as it is with paradox—is the principal context in which to sharpen our spiritual senses. The mere fact of gathering with others on the Lord's Day reminds us that the Holy Spirit continuously draws together what evil strives to scatter. In congregational worship, we hear God's word to us; recall how lavishly God loves us; see this love enacted in baptism; taste its sweetness and its wonder in the Lord's Supper; and take stock of our response to it in confession, hymn and corporate prayer. Small groups given to prayer, study or outreach also offer places to increase our awareness of the Holy Spirit's leading. In the company of faithful seekers, another person's moment of vulnerability, a truth spoken in love or a story told in trust can awaken insight into ways the Holy Spirit is also present with us. Family life, which Martin Luther placed ahead of the monastery as the true school of charity, provides many opportunities to learn the art of self-forgetfulness. *Time spent with the poor and needy instructs us in our own poverty,* prepares us to receive more than we bestow from those who often seem so distressingly different and gives the Spirit occasion to teach us the extent of our common humanity.

Personal spiritual practices also prime us to be responsive to the Holy Spirit's approach. The meditative reading of scripture encouraged in this Bible enables us to become at home in God's word. As this occurs, we develop a growing familiarity with the Holy Spirit who fashioned and continues to dwell in holy writ. According to twelfth-century Cistercian abbot Peter of Celle, such reading is nothing less than "the soul's food, light, lamp, refuge, consolation, and the spice of every spiritual savor." *Prayer, that royal road to deepening intimacy with God, will inevitably acquaint us with the guiding grace of the Spirit.* It is in the Spirit that we pray and through the Spirit that the inarticulate yearnings of our heart receive coherent expression before God (see Romans 8:27). Various "spiritual fitness" exercises, including abstaining from self-destructive activities and attitudes, allocating personal resources in a godly manner and following simple rules of life, help to *remind us that God is the center of each day.* Such exercises produce stamina for continued acceptance of the Holy Spirit's invitation to "come and follow."

Following the leading of the Holy Spirit builds in us a growing capacity for extraordinary witness to God's kingdom, such as extending forgiveness where there has been genuine injury. It also reinforces in us the knowledge that *our new humanity in Jesus Christ is the work of the Spirit and not our own achievement.* In our human weakness, we need the strength and sustenance of the Holy Spirit to maintain the Godward direction of our life. Such assistance is clearly promised by Jesus: "When he, the Spirit of truth, comes, he will guide you into all truth" (John 16:13). This truth is what the author of Ephesians calls "the fullness of Christ" (Ephesians 4:13). The measure of this truth is nothing other than love. *Love is the first gift of the Spirit and the final test of our freedom in Jesus Christ* (see 1 Corinthians 13; Galatians 5:22; Colossians 1:8). All other marks of our new humanity—joy, peace, patience, kindness, generosity, faithfulness, self-control—are manifestations of this love, a love that binds us to Jesus Christ in the unity of the Holy Spirit for the sake of the world God loves so much. "Since we live by the Spirit, let us keep in step with the Spirit" (Galatians 5:25).

IN THE WORLD

In a life increasingly given to the guidance of the Holy Spirit, our new humanity in Jesus Christ gradually becomes more visible and effective in the world. Far from removing us from the messiness of the world, *spiritual formation plunges us into the middle of the world's rage and suffering.* It was to this place of pain and bewilderment that Jesus Christ was sent as the visible image of the invisible God (see John 14:9; Colossians 1:15). It was to this place of bitterness and infirmity that Jesus Christ was sent, not to condemn but to save (see John 3:17). Those who are being formed in his image take the same path. Love, the full measure of Christian maturity, impels us with kindly urgency in this direction. *Love desires to be seen, known and received, for by these actions it grows wider and deeper.* Through us love is extended to the furthest recesses of human sorrow and need. Thus, God's love for the world—in us because we are in Jesus Christ—becomes a sign of hope and a source of transformation in the world.

"No one is richer, no one more powerful, no one more free," observed Thomas à Kempis, "than *the person who can give his whole life to God and freely serve others with deep humility and love.*" To embody in thought, word and deed the love of God made known in our Lord Jesus Christ is the signal mark of faithful discipleship, the inexhaustible strength of vital congregations and the ultimate goal of spiritual formation.

—John Mogabgab

Meeting God in

Scripture

IN EVERY ERA, in myriad places and in all kinds of circumstances, people have testified that the Bible speaks powerfully—that the Word of God can and does change lives. But perhaps you feel that your own experience with reading the Bible pales in significance when compared to such a standard. You feel like the woman who confessed, *"Surely there has to be a way to get more out of my Bible reading!"* Your times with the Bible yield much of value and interest—but transformation? That is another matter. You learn facts—places and names—but have yet to hear God's voice. As much as you value the insights gained, you long to meet God.

When you read and study scripture *it is possible to grow beyond an intellectual knowledge of the Bible to the transformation of your heart.* The Bible can become "a lamp to [your] feet and a light for [your] path" (Ps. 119:105). You can go to the heart of the matter and meet the Author. The eighteenth-century bishop Tikhon of Zodonsk articulated well what can happen: "Whenever you read the Gospel," he wrote, "Christ Himself is speaking to you. And while you read, you are praying and talking to Him." Reading and studying the Bible can become more fulfilling than anything you have previously experienced.

But how? Providentially we are heirs to several helpful approaches. The great spiritual writers of the past have given us a legacy that engages mind and heart, intellect and will. They have suggested ways that help us derive life from the text and so become agents of life for others.

In the history of Christian spirituality, the oldest and best-known approach to Bible reading is called "spiritual reading" or "divine reading" (the Latin is *lectio divina*). The practice dates back to at least the fourth century, but the idea behind it is even more ancient. Spiritual reading entails a fourfold approach:

First, read slowly. Choose a relatively short passage of a biblical book (no more than several paragraphs or a short chapter), and read meditatively, prayerfully. In this phase you are a seeker looking for the "word within the Word." **Watch for a key phrase or word that jumps out at you** or promises to have special meaning for you. Concern yourself not so much with the amount you are reading as the depth with which you read. It is better to dwell profoundly on one word or phrase than to skim the surface of several chapters. **Read with your own life and choices in view,** recalling Paul's injunction that God's word is "useful for teaching, for reproof, for correction, and for training in righteousness" (2 Tim. 3:16).

Second, meditate. Christian meditation is not stream of consciousness or free association, nor is it Eastern transcendental meditation. Rather, **it is letting a special word or phrase that you discovered in the first phase of reading sink into your heart.** It is what the biblical writers had in mind when they spoke of "meditating" on the Book of the Law "day and night" (Josh. 1:8; Ps. 1:2). For example, when you are reading Psalm 23, perhaps you linger at the phrase, "The Lord is my shepherd." For reasons that may not be immediately apparent, the word *my* stands out. You are struck by the idea that God can be—and wants to be—your shepherd. In this second phase of spiritual reading, stay with that thought. Use whatever study skills and related materials that are available to you to enrich your reflection. **Bring mind, will, and emotions to the enterprise.** This meditative stage is comparable to walking around a great statue, viewing it from multiple vantage points. You are like Mary, Jesus' mother, who heard of the angel's announcement and "treasured up" and "pondered" what she had heard (Luke 2:19).

Third, pray the text. You have listened; now you respond—that is, **you form a prayer that expresses your response to the idea.** You "pray it back to God." You are, in effect, engaging God in dialogue. In the case of "The Lord is my shepherd," your response could easily be a prayer of gratitude. It might be a prolonged recollection of all of the ways that God has been present with you over the years, shepherding you through life. This phase of divine reading is in reality not separate from the other aspects but flows through all of them, so that *you are continually converting the text into a prayer*, a prayer formed by God's revealed will. What you have read is woven through what you tell God. You thereby acknowledge that God's Word "shall not return . . . empty, but it shall accomplish that which [God desires]" (Isa. 55:11).

Fourth, contemplate. That is, rest. In divine reading you eventually arrive at the place at which you no longer work on the text but allow it to work itself into you. *You let it soak into your deepest being.* You are not straining for additional insights; you simply are savoring an encounter—with God's truth and with God's own self. You enjoy the rest that Jesus promised those who come to him (see Matthew 11:28). Quietly, when ready, move toward the moment in which you *ask God to show you how to live out what you have experienced.*

Spiritual reading enables God to "speak and show" in ways that transform the written word into a living Word—just for you. Then, having "taste[d] and see[n] that the LORD is good" (Psalm 34:8), *you move outward in daily living to become a blessing to others.*

IGNATIAN READING

Attributed to Ignatius of Loyola (1491–1556) and articulated in his "Spiritual Exercises," the Ignatian method of reading the Bible likewise invites us to enter actively and fully into the text. *It encourages detachment from either ego-driven success or fear-motivated anxiety*, leaving the soul free to obey God's stirrings.

Generally, Ignatian reading works best with narrative material in which actual characters lived a story of faith. The idea is to *place yourself into the text as a careful observer—* a "fly on the wall," if you will. Ignatius commended the use of the five senses in such meditation. You taste, hear, see, smell, and feel your way through the passage. Occasionally you become one of the characters, seeing the story unfold from his or her viewpoint. Most of all, the aim is to help you *perceive the narrative from the viewpoint of Jesus so that you may more fully participate in his mind, heart, and work.*

For the sake of practice, you might like to concentrate on John 18:1-11 and spend five days reading it. Each day, imagine yourself as a different one of the characters: Judas, a soldier, Peter, the high priest's servant, or Jesus. As you enter vicariously into the position of each character, *ask God to teach you how to live in greater fidelity and obedience—* which is the ultimate aim of the Ignatian method of reading scripture and of Ignatian spirituality in general.

While not a direct by-product of the teachings of Francis of Assisi, Franciscan reading exhibits primary qualities of Franciscan spirituality, such as action, spontaneity, love, praise, beauty, and delight in creation. Like Ignatian reflection, Franciscan reading involves the mental process of entering personally into the text. But this method is more fluid. *It allows the encounter with God to incorporate ordinary activities and daily experiences.*

For example, turn in your Bible to Isaiah 53 and read through this chapter. To help you enter into its message and reflect on Jesus' sacrificial death on the cross, the Franciscan method would invite you to take actions such as these: If you have a model of a cross with Jesus on it, you might hold it in your hand, gazing at the details of the Lord's crucified body. You might sing a hymn such as "O Sacred Head, Now Wounded" or "The Old Rugged Cross." You might look through today's newspaper and identify places in the world where people are suffering. You might write a poem or paint a picture to capture what you are thinking and feeling. In the Franciscan spirit, you would express your emotions through an activity. You would be encouraged to "feel" something of what Jesus experienced on your behalf. You would saturate the entire experience with prayer, *asking God to make you an instrument of peace* in the lives of those who are suffering.

To be sure, these methods do not exhaust our options for formative reading. You might use the fruit of the Spirit described in Galatians 5:22–23 as a lens through which you read, asking yourself how a particular passage might deepen love, joy, peace, patience, kindness, goodness, gentleness, faithfulness, and self-control in your life. You might use what some have called the Fivefold Question (What does this passage say about God's nature? What does it say about human nature? What does it say about how God relates to people? What does it suggest about how I might pray? What does it suggest about how I might act?).

Whatever method you use at any given time, adopt an underlying attitude of openness to seeking truth. We pray for a "scriptural mind" that is obedient, faithful to the historic Christian tradition, Christ-centered and personal. *We must desire to find truth and be willing to apply it to our own lives* and our relationships with others. Apart from such foundational commitments, any method becomes mere technique. With them, any of the methods of reading scripture can become a true means of grace.

—J. Steven Harper

Meeting God in

Community

WE WERE NOT CREATED to live in isolation. No person "is an island, entire of itself," wrote the poet John Donne. While no one questions the need for periods of solitude and refreshment in our lives, faith tends to thrive most readily when shared with others. *Without the connections community affords us, we experience what someone once called "spiritual loneliness."* For we meet God not just as we sit alone in quiet corners but in and through the people with whom we live, work and interact as we go through our daily routine.

Relationships present us with both a remarkable privilege and an awesome responsibility. Proverbs 27:17 tells us that "as iron sharpens iron, so one [person] sharpens [and shapes] another," (NIV). *As other people's lives touch ours, they help to form our faith and make us who we are.* As we touch others, we reflect God's love to them.

Relationships with other believers have extraordinary power in our lives because Jesus is present in them. *Jesus knew the importance of people in conveying God's grace and presence.* "Where two or three are gathered in my name," he said, "I am there among them" (Matt. 18:20). Within our churches, small groups, families, and friendships, we learn from one another. We find encouragement. We challenge one another to follow God more faithfully. Other Christians enable us to walk as we should when we might otherwise have strayed or wandered. *God uses relationships to form us, and relationships form us so that God can use us.*

POWER FOR GROWTH AND CHANGE

The Bible offers many examples of the formational power of relationships. The story of Ruth and Naomi demonstrates how the presence of other believers can enable us to do what we can't do alone. Ruth is a foreigner, a Moabite who has married Naomi's son. When Naomi's husband and her sons (including Ruth's husband) die, she grieves, saying, "The hand of the LORD has turned against me!" (Ruth 1:13). Ruth, also widowed, chooses to stay with Naomi rather than return to her own kin. Ruth speaks the words that are well-known and much-loved: "Where you go I will go; and where you lodge, I will lodge; your people shall be my people, and your God my God" (Ruth 1:16). Just think of the magnitude of the change those words brought about! Something in this relationship makes Ruth willing to leave her family and country to adopt Naomi's faith. The younger woman seeks guidance from Naomi and in turn cares for her. Their loving relationship releases Naomi from the bitterness of her losses and draws Ruth into relationship with the God of Israel. Eventually Ruth becomes the ancestor of Jesus the Messiah (see Matthew 1:5).

Elijah and Elisha offer an example of the way God uses the power of relationships to build strong leaders. *God, employing Elijah as Elisha's mentor, makes a dramatic difference in the life of the younger man who is eager to serve God faithfully.* Elijah, a famous prophet, is near the end of his ministry when God tells him to seek out and anoint Elisha as his successor. Elijah throws his cloak over Elisha's shoulders as the younger man walks behind his plow and oxen, publicly calling Elisha to a new way of life. What a dramatic act! Elisha leaves his farm work to become Elijah's attendant (see 1 Kings 19:16-21), following the prophet and seeking to learn from him. He refuses to leave his mentor and asks for "a double portion" of the spirit that has made Elijah great (see 2 Kings 2:9). One man is clearly the teacher and the other the student, and, like Elijah, *Elisha acknowledges that God is at the center of his life and ministry.* Through his relationship with Elijah, he develops the courage, faith and skills to carry on the work of the prophet as God's spokesman.

In the New Testament Mary and Elizabeth offer us yet another example of how relationships help us mature in faith. *Their relationship illustrates the value of sharing mutual insight and encouragement.* According to the Gospel of Luke, young Mary is visited by the angel Gabriel, who tells her that she will bear a son who will be the Messiah. Mary, "much perplexed by his words" (Luke 1:29), hurries to visit her older cousin Elizabeth, who is also pregnant. Though Mary has told the angel that she wants to be obedient to God's will, she is surely also confused and frightened. But after Elizabeth speaks to her, Mary breaks into a song of praise to God; her faith has been strengthened. Mary spends three months with Elizabeth, who supports her and in turn is supported in the joyful yet sacrificial work to which God has called both of them. Mary discovered, as many have, that *when we are hesitant to face what lies ahead, spending time with someone who knows us and shares our faith can help us see more clearly* and understand more deeply the issues we need to deal with. It fortifies us to move forward in faith.

SOUL FRIENDS

Throughout the history of the church, writers and leaders have echoed this message. In the twelfth century, Aelred of Rievaulx said that Christian friendship can be "a step to raise us to the love and knowledge of God." He also spoke of the joy of having a friend with "whom you need have no fear to confess your failings; one to whom you can unblushingly make known what progress you have made in the spiritual life; one to whom you can entrust all the secrets of your heart and before whom you can place all your plans." Teresa of Avila wrote in the sixteenth century of how "it is a great advantage for us to be able to consult someone who knows us, so that we may learn to know ourselves." John Wesley went so far as to declare that there is no such thing as a solitary Christian.

What these Christians from various times and places learned is that *God uses close and continuing relationships to form us into the image of Jesus.* As we share both our high moments and our low, pray for one another, help each other and work together toward common goals, we reflect Jesus and acknowledge Jesus' presence with us.

NURTURING YOUR OWN SOUL FRIENDS

To begin to meet God in community you may want to reach out to other believers with whom you can discuss your spiritual journey. Such conversation helps you sort out what you know about yourself and about God. It may be especially valuable if this action is deliberate. Ask one or two mature individuals with whom you can exchange thoughts and prayers with confidence and assurance of confidentiality to meet with you. This practice has traditionally been called "spiritual guidance," "spiritual direction" or "spiritual friendship." This kind of conversation may also occur in the context of worship services, church school classes, and small groups. One-on-one relationships and small groups allow for a depth of interaction not possible in larger, more formal settings. They allow us to pray aloud for one another with potentially life-changing results. As Alan Jones, an essayist on Christian friendship, stated, "We cannot help but tremble on the brink of surrender, but it is our companions who give us the courage to jump."

SPEND TIME OBSERVING THE LIVES OF FAITHFUL CHRISTIANS

The New Testament tells us repeatedly that *we become like Jesus by spending time with those who are his friends.* We look at those who have led us, consider the outcome of their faith and then choose to imitate them (see Hebrews 13:7). Some find it a good discipline to think periodically about someone whose faith they admire. Consider approaching one or more such people to ask them how God has been at work in their lives. (For biblical examples of this process, see 1 Corinthians 4:6; Philippians 3:17; 1 Thessalonians 1:6; and 2 Thessalonians 3:9.)

STAY ACTIVE IN A CHURCH COMMUNITY

 As happens within our immediate family circle, when we rub shoulders with others we are continually confronted with reminders of our weaknesses and brokenness. We wound others and are wounded by them. Romans 12:18 acknowledges that living with others can be difficult, urging, "If it is possible, so far as it depends on you, live peaceably with all." While imperfections abound within what Paul calls "the body of Christ," *God still uses the company of believers to grace our lives and transform the world* (see Romans 12:4-5; 1 Corinthians 12:12; Ephesians 5:30). We cannot do without our fellow believers. "Let us not give up meeting together," the writer of the letter to the Hebrews urges (10:25, NIV). At their best, relationships with other believers not only shield us in difficult times but also help us to confront our imperfections. We find a place to mutually speak "the truth in love" (Eph. 4:15).

VIEW YOUR INVOLVEMENT WITH OTHER BELIEVERS AS AN OPPORTUNITY TO HELP

It is a privilege to nurture another person, to be trusted to hear another's dreams and concerns, to pray for someone. In so doing we may discover myriad ways to use the gifts that God has given us to benefit our family in Christ as well as for our own growth and enjoyment. As we help others, we too will be helped. As we comfort and teach and encourage, we will be comforted, taught, and encouraged in turn. As we experience community, we find our lives enriched, in turn providing us with more to give to others.

—MARY LOU REDDING

Notes

Introduction

1. The process for group *lectio* as outlined is based on Norvene Vest's book *Gathered in the Word: Praying the Scripture in Small Groups* (Nashville, TN: Upper Room Books, 1996). You may want to read Vest's book for an account of how different people respond to this way of reading scripture, but that is not necessary to the process.

Session 4

1. Adapted in part from *Prayer, Fear, and Our Powers: Finding Our Healing, Release, and Growth in Christ* by Flora Slosson Wuellner (Nashville, TN: Upper Room Books, 1989), 118–20 and in part from a meditation led by Marjorie Thompson at the Cooperative Baptist Fellowship gathering on 27 June 2003, as part of a presentation titled "Being the Presence of Christ Globally."

About the Author

Mary Lou Redding's

absolute favorite book in the world to read is the Bible, whose Old Testament characters feel like personal friends. She has read their stories so many times that the characters have become part of her personal history; she sees herself in their struggles and acknowledges their weaknesses as her own. Her fascination with God's using such imperfect and, at times, unwilling people to accomplish divine purposes makes her consider that God might use even her.

Redding has a Master of Arts degree in Rhetoric and Writing and has worked professionally as a writer and editor for many years. She helped to create and was a contributor to *The Spiritual Formation Bible* and has published a number of books with Upper Room: *Breaking and Mending: Divorce and God's Grace, While We Wait: Living the Questions of Advent,* and *The Power of a Focused Heart,* a small-group study of the Beatitudes. She experiences God's grace and presence and serves within the community of faith at Brentwood United Methodist Church in Brentwood, Tennessee.